Machine Learning with Python: Build Your First AI Model

A Step-by-Step Guide to Using Python for Machine Learning Projects

MIGUEL FARMER

RAFAEL SANDERS

Table of Content

TABLE OF CONTENTS

INTRODUCTION

Machine Learning with Python: Build Your First AI Model

In today's data-driven world, machine learning (ML) and artificial intelligence (AI) are transforming industries, businesses, and everyday life. From personalized recommendations on streaming platforms to self-driving cars and predictive healthcare, machine learning is the backbone of innovations that were once considered science fiction. However, despite the enormous potential and rapid growth of these fields, many aspiring data scientists and engineers still find themselves intimidated by the complexity and technical nature of machine learning concepts.

This book, **"Machine Learning with Python: Build Your First AI Model,"** is designed to bridge the gap between theoretical concepts and practical implementation, providing an accessible yet thorough guide to understanding and building machine learning models using Python. Whether you're a complete beginner or someone looking to deepen your knowledge, this book will guide you through the essentials of machine learning in a hands-on and straightforward manner. By the end, you'll have the skills to build, evaluate, and deploy your own machine learning models.

Why This Book?

Machine learning is a vast and multifaceted field that spans a variety of techniques, from supervised and unsupervised learning to deep learning and reinforcement learning. The journey to becoming proficient in machine learning can often feel overwhelming, but **this book is specifically crafted to make learning accessible, interactive, and most importantly, fun.**

Throughout the book, you will:

- Learn the **fundamentals of machine learning**, including key concepts such as data preprocessing, model evaluation, and optimization.
- Master how to use **Python libraries** like **Pandas, NumPy, Scikit-Learn,** and **Matplotlib** to implement machine learning algorithms.
- Explore practical, real-world **hands-on projects** that demonstrate how machine learning can be applied to solve common challenges in data analysis, prediction, and classification.
- Understand how to evaluate, tune, and optimize models to ensure that they not only perform well on your data but also generalize to new, unseen data.

Unlike many technical textbooks, this guide emphasizes **practical implementation** over theory, ensuring that you walk away with real, applicable skills that you can use immediately in your own projects. Along the way, you will encounter a variety of exercises and examples designed to reinforce your learning and give you the confidence to tackle more advanced machine learning tasks.

What You Will Learn

The book is structured to gradually introduce machine learning concepts and techniques, starting with simple algorithms and progressing to more advanced topics. Key learning outcomes include:

- **Understanding the Basics of Machine Learning**: We'll begin by defining machine learning, discussing its various types (supervised, unsupervised, reinforcement learning), and explaining key concepts such as features, labels, and models. You'll also learn about the different types of problems that machine learning can solve, such as classification, regression, clustering, and recommendation systems.
- **Preprocessing Data**: One of the most important aspects of any machine learning project is ensuring that the data you use is clean, consistent, and ready for training. This book will teach you how to preprocess data, including handling missing values, normalizing features, encoding categorical variables, and splitting your data into training and testing sets.

8

- **Building Your First Model**: You will be introduced to basic machine learning algorithms like **linear regression, logistic regression,** and **k-nearest neighbors (KNN)**. You'll learn how to train these models, make predictions, and evaluate their performance.

- **Model Evaluation and Improvement**: After building your models, we'll explore how to evaluate them using metrics like accuracy, precision, recall, F1-score, and the confusion matrix. You'll also learn techniques for improving model performance, including hyperparameter tuning, feature selection, and cross-validation.

- **Advanced Topics**: For those who are ready to dive deeper, this book also introduces more complex machine learning techniques like **decision trees, random forests, neural networks,** and **deep learning**. You'll understand how these models work and how to implement them using Python.

- **Deployment and Real-World Applications**: The final sections of the book cover **model deployment**, showing you how to take your trained model and integrate it into a real-world application. You'll learn how to deploy models using frameworks like **Flask** or **FastAPI**, making your models accessible through APIs.

Who Should Read This Book?

This book is aimed at anyone interested in machine learning and artificial intelligence, regardless of their prior experience. If you are a:

- **Beginner in Data Science**: This book is perfect for those who have no prior experience in machine learning. The explanations are clear, and each concept is backed by practical examples and code snippets, making complex ideas more understandable.
- **Intermediate Learner Looking to Build Models**: If you've already explored some basic machine learning concepts and want to apply them in real projects, this book will help you take your skills to the next level, offering hands-on examples of building and deploying models.
- **Python Developer Wanting to Learn Machine Learning**: If you already have experience with Python and want to use it for machine learning, this book will teach you how to apply Python to solve machine learning problems.
- **Data Analyst or Engineer Seeking Practical Skills**: If you're working in data analysis or engineering and want to broaden your skill set by learning machine learning techniques, this book provides a practical, application-focused approach.

How to Use This Book

This book is designed to be read sequentially, building upon the concepts and techniques introduced in earlier chapters. However, if you're more experienced, you can skip ahead to chapters that focus on specific techniques or tools. Each chapter includes practical examples and code that you can run on your machine, making it easy to apply the concepts directly.

Additionally, the book is full of **exercises** at the end of each chapter, allowing you to practice what you've learned. You can also find solutions to the exercises in the appendices, ensuring that you can check your understanding and gain more insight into the problem-solving process.

Final Thoughts

Machine learning is a journey, not a destination. With this book as your guide, you will develop the essential skills needed to build, optimize, and deploy machine learning models using Python. Whether you're aiming to become a data scientist, enhance your AI knowledge, or simply explore the field, this book provides the foundation you need to succeed.

The world of machine learning is dynamic and full of possibilities. As you work through the chapters and complete the projects, you'll gain confidence in your ability to tackle real-world machine learning challenges. So, get ready to dive in, experiment, and see how the power of machine learning can be harnessed to solve problems and innovate across various domains.

Welcome to your machine learning journey!

CHAPTER 1

INTRODUCTION TO MACHINE LEARNING

What is Machine Learning?

Machine learning is a subset of artificial intelligence (AI) that focuses on building systems that can learn from and make decisions based on data. In traditional programming, the programmer writes explicit instructions for the computer to follow. However, in machine learning, the system learns patterns from data and improves its performance over time without being explicitly programmed to do so. This ability to improve automatically is what differentiates machine learning from traditional coding.

At its core, machine learning uses statistical techniques to enable computers to "learn" from past experiences or historical data, without direct programming for every specific task. The goal is for the model to make predictions or decisions based on input data.

Overview of Machine Learning vs. Traditional Programming

Traditional programming relies on humans writing explicit instructions for the computer to follow. For example, if you want to calculate the total sum of a list of numbers, you'd write code to loop through the list, add the numbers together, and return the result.

On the other hand, in machine learning, instead of writing specific instructions for every possible scenario, you feed data into a model and allow it to learn patterns on its own. The system then uses these learned patterns to make decisions or predictions about new, unseen data. The key difference is that in machine learning, the system adapts over time as it gets exposed to more data, while in traditional programming, the logic is fixed unless manually changed by the programmer.

Consider the example of spam email detection:

- **Traditional programming** would involve writing rules (e.g., if an email contains certain words, it's spam).
- **Machine learning** would involve training a model on a large dataset of emails, where the system learns the characteristics of spam emails (based on past examples) and can then predict whether new emails are spam or not without needing explicit rules for every case.

Key Types of Machine Learning

Machine learning can be broadly categorized into three main types, each used in different situations and for solving different kinds of problems:

1. **Supervised Learning**

   o **Definition**: Supervised learning is the most common type of machine learning. In this approach, a model is trained on a labeled dataset, meaning the data has both input features and the corresponding correct output (known as labels).

   o **Example**: A classic example is email classification, where the training data consists of labeled emails (spam or not) and features like the sender, subject, and content. The model learns to map these features to the correct label and can later classify new emails.

   o **Key Algorithms**: Linear regression, decision trees, support vector machines, and k-nearest neighbors.

2. **Unsupervised Learning**

   o **Definition**: In unsupervised learning, the algorithm works with unlabeled data, meaning the system tries to find structure or patterns without explicit guidance on what the output should look like.

   o **Example**: A common application is customer segmentation in marketing, where unsupervised learning can group customers into clusters based on purchasing behavior or demographics, without needing predefined labels.

- o **Key Algorithms**: K-means clustering, hierarchical clustering, principal component analysis (PCA).

3. **Reinforcement Learning**
   - o **Definition**: Reinforcement learning is based on the concept of agents that take actions in an environment to maximize a cumulative reward. The agent learns through trial and error, adjusting its actions based on feedback (rewards or penalties).
   - o **Example**: A self-driving car is a good example, where the car (the agent) learns how to navigate traffic by taking actions (driving forward, turning, stopping) and receiving feedback based on the success of those actions (e.g., staying in the lane or avoiding collisions).
   - o **Key Algorithms**: Q-learning, deep Q-networks (DQN), and policy gradients.

Importance of Machine Learning in the Real World

Machine learning has transformed industries and continues to shape the way businesses and individuals operate. Its applications are vast, spanning a wide range of sectors and improving efficiency, decision-making, and user experiences. Some real-world examples include:

16

- **Healthcare**: Machine learning algorithms help doctors diagnose diseases, analyze medical images, and even predict patient outcomes. For instance, models are used to detect tumors in radiology scans or predict the likelihood of a disease based on patient data.

- **Finance**: Machine learning is used for fraud detection, risk analysis, and algorithmic trading. Financial institutions analyze transaction data to spot unusual patterns and prevent fraud.

- **Retail and E-Commerce**: Online stores use machine learning to recommend products based on user behavior, personalizing the shopping experience. This boosts sales by suggesting items customers are most likely to buy.

- **Transportation**: Ride-sharing companies like Uber and Lyft use machine learning to predict demand, optimize routes, and set dynamic pricing. Self-driving cars also rely on machine learning to make real-time decisions on the road.

- **Entertainment**: Streaming services like Netflix and Spotify use machine learning to recommend movies, TV shows, and music based on user preferences and behavior.

In all these examples, machine learning models help make better, faster decisions and automate tasks that would traditionally require human input. Its ability to analyze large amounts of data and recognize patterns makes it invaluable across sectors, driving innovation and improving overall performance.

This chapter lays the groundwork for understanding the essentials of machine learning, comparing it with traditional programming, and introducing the key types of machine learning. It also highlights the importance of machine learning in real-world applications, helping to set the stage for deeper exploration in subsequent chapters.

CHAPTER 2

GETTING STARTED WITH PYTHON FOR MACHINE LEARNING

Installing Python and Necessary Libraries

Before diving into machine learning, the first step is setting up the Python environment on your computer. Python is widely used for machine learning due to its simplicity and the vast array of libraries that support data manipulation, visualization, and machine learning tasks.

1. **Installing Python**
   - Python can be downloaded from the official website: https://www.python.org/downloads/.
   - For most users, the recommended version is the latest stable release (Python 3.x). Ensure that you check the option to "Add Python to PATH" during installation.

2. **Installing Anaconda (Optional but Recommended)**
   - Anaconda is a popular Python distribution that simplifies package management and deployment, particularly for data science and machine learning

projects. It comes pre-installed with most of the libraries needed for machine learning.

o Download Anaconda from https://www.anaconda.com/products/individual.

o After installing Anaconda, you can manage packages and environments easily using the `conda` command in the terminal.

3. **Installing Libraries** Once Python or Anaconda is installed, you need to install specific libraries to start working with machine learning. Here are the most common libraries:

o **Pandas**: For data manipulation and analysis.

```bash
pip install pandas
```

o **NumPy**: For numerical computing and handling arrays.

```bash
pip install numpy
```

o **Matplotlib**: For plotting and visualizing data.

```bash
pip install matplotlib
```

- o **Scikit-learn**: For machine learning algorithms and tools.

```bash
pip install scikit-learn
```

- o **TensorFlow**: For deep learning and neural networks (useful for more advanced models).

```bash
pip install tensorflow
```

Setting Up Your Development Environment

Once the necessary libraries are installed, it's time to choose and set up your development environment. A good development environment makes it easier to write, test, and debug your code.

1. **Jupyter Notebooks**
   - o Jupyter Notebooks provide an interactive environment where you can write Python code, run it, and visualize the results all in the same place. It's widely used for data science and machine learning due to its flexibility and ease of use.
   - o To install Jupyter, use the following command:

```bash
```

```
pip install notebook
```

o   Once installed, you can start a notebook by running:

```bash
```

```
jupyter notebook
```

o   This will open a new tab in your web browser where you can create and edit Python files in the form of cells, which you can execute interactively. You can also visualize data with inline charts and graphs, making it ideal for exploring machine learning models.

2. **Integrated Development Environments (IDEs)**

o   If you prefer working in a more traditional environment, Python IDEs offer powerful features like code completion, debugging tools, and project management. Some popular Python IDEs for machine learning include:

- **PyCharm**: A feature-rich IDE that offers many tools for writing and testing Python code, with support for machine learning libraries and tools.

22

- **VS Code**: A lightweight yet powerful IDE with great support for Python. You can install extensions like Python and Jupyter for an enhanced experience.
- **Spyder**: A Python IDE specifically designed for data science and scientific computing, offering a console and variable explorer.

3. **Virtual Environments**

   o Using virtual environments is a good practice to keep your project dependencies isolated from the global Python environment. This ensures that the libraries used in one project don't interfere with others.

   o To create a virtual environment, use the following commands:

```bash
python -m venv myenv
```

   o To activate the environment (on Windows):

```bash
myenv\Scripts\activate
```

   o To activate on macOS or Linux:

```bash
bash
```

```bash
source myenv/bin/activate
```

Overview of Python Libraries for Machine Learning

Python offers a wide variety of libraries that make machine learning tasks easier. Here are some of the most important libraries you'll use throughout your journey.

1. **Pandas**
   o **Purpose**: Data manipulation and analysis.
   o **Key Features**: Pandas provides data structures like DataFrames, which are perfect for handling structured data (e.g., tables, CSV files, databases). You can easily load, manipulate, and analyze data using functions like `groupby()`, `merge()`, and `pivot_table()`.
   o **Example Usage**:

   ```python
   python
   ```

   ```python
   import pandas as pd
   df = pd.read_csv('data.csv')  # Load
   a dataset
   df.head()  # Display the first few
   rows of the dataframe
   ```

2. **NumPy**

- o **Purpose**: Numerical computing and handling arrays.

- o **Key Features**: NumPy provides support for large multi-dimensional arrays and matrices, as well as a collection of mathematical functions to operate on these arrays. It's essential for handling data in machine learning models, especially when dealing with large datasets or performing mathematical operations.

- o **Example Usage**:

```python
import numpy as np
arr = np.array([1, 2, 3, 4, 5])
print(arr.mean())    # Calculate the mean of the array
```

3. **Scikit-learn**

- o **Purpose**: Machine learning algorithms and tools.

- o **Key Features**: Scikit-learn is one of the most popular libraries for machine learning in Python. It provides simple and efficient tools for data mining and data analysis. It includes algorithms for classification, regression, clustering, and dimensionality reduction.

- o **Example Usage**:

```
python
```

```
from sklearn.model_selection import
train_test_split
from sklearn.linear_model import
LogisticRegression
X_train, X_test, y_train, y_test =
train_test_split(X,               y,
test_size=0.2)
model = LogisticRegression()
model.fit(X_train, y_train)
```

4. **TensorFlow**

   o **Purpose**: Deep learning and neural networks.

   o **Key Features**: TensorFlow is an open-source library developed by Google for deep learning applications. It allows you to build and train complex neural networks with a high level of flexibility. While it has a steeper learning curve than Scikit-learn, it's incredibly powerful for working with large-scale machine learning tasks, especially in deep learning and AI projects.

   o **Example Usage**:

```
python
```

```
import tensorflow as tf
model = tf.keras.Sequential([
```

```
    tf.keras.layers.Dense(128,
activation='relu',
input_shape=(784,)),
    tf.keras.layers.Dense(10,
activation='softmax')
])
model.compile(optimizer='adam',
loss='sparse_categorical_crossentro
py', metrics=['accuracy'])
```

Conclusion

Setting up the right development environment is the foundation for any machine learning project. In this chapter, we've covered how to install Python and the necessary libraries, set up Jupyter Notebooks and IDEs, and provided an overview of key libraries like Pandas, NumPy, Scikit-learn, and TensorFlow. With this setup, you're now ready to start working with machine learning models in Python, and the next chapters will guide you through the process of building your first models and applying these tools effectively.

CHAPTER 3

UNDERSTANDING THE BASICS OF DATA

The Importance of Data in Machine Learning

In machine learning, data is the foundation. It's the fuel that drives the learning process. Without data, machine learning models cannot "learn" anything meaningful. The quality, quantity, and relevance of the data you use directly affect the performance of your models. Essentially, machine learning is all about identifying patterns and making predictions based on historical data.

Why is data so important?

- **Learning from Patterns**: Machine learning algorithms use data to identify patterns, which then enable them to make predictions or decisions on new, unseen data. Without enough or the right kind of data, the model may not learn the correct patterns, leading to poor performance.

- **Model Accuracy**: The better the quality of the data, the more accurate the machine learning model will be. A clean, well-labeled dataset with representative examples leads to a more reliable model.

- **Real-World Impact**: In real-world applications, like healthcare, finance, or e-commerce, data-driven models can lead to better decisions, higher efficiency, and improved outcomes. For instance, predicting customer behavior in e-commerce or diagnosing diseases from medical data.

Types of Data

Understanding the types of data is crucial for effective machine learning. Data can be categorized into different types, and the way it is handled varies depending on the category.

1. **Structured Data**
   - **Definition**: Structured data is highly organized and typically stored in tabular form, such as in spreadsheets or databases. It consists of rows and columns, with each column representing a specific attribute or feature, and each row representing an individual data point or observation.
   - **Example**: Customer information in a database, like name, age, income, and purchase history.
   - **Characteristics**:
     - Easy to analyze and process using traditional data analysis tools like SQL.

- Fits well with most machine learning algorithms (especially supervised learning algorithms).

o **Usage in Machine Learning**: Structured data is commonly used in regression, classification, and clustering tasks.

o **Example Dataset**:

Customer ID	Age	Income	Purchased Product
1	25	50,000	Laptop
2	40	75,000	Phone
3	30	60,000	Tablet

2. **Unstructured Data**

o **Definition**: Unstructured data is data that doesn't have a predefined format or structure. It is often text-heavy, such as social media posts, audio files, images, and videos.

o **Example**: A collection of tweets, product reviews, or medical imaging data.

o **Characteristics**:

- Harder to store, manage, and analyze using traditional tools.

- Requires advanced techniques (e.g., Natural Language Processing for text or convolutional neural networks for images) to process and analyze.

  o **Usage in Machine Learning**: Unstructured data is common in deep learning applications, such as sentiment analysis (text) or image classification (images).

  o **Example Dataset**:
    - Text: "This product is great, I love it!"
    - Image: A photograph of a cat.

3. **Semi-Structured Data**

   o **Definition**: Semi-structured data falls between structured and unstructured data. It doesn't have a fixed schema but still contains some organization, such as tags or markers that make it easier to analyze.

   o **Example**: JSON files or XML documents, where data is organized in a way that allows some elements to be easily identified.

   o **Characteristics**:
     - More flexible than structured data but easier to analyze than unstructured data.
     - Often used for web data (e.g., logs, XML, JSON).

o **Usage in Machine Learning**: Semi-structured data can be useful for tasks that involve extracting information from sources like APIs, web scraping, or processing large text-based datasets.

How Data is Collected and Preprocessed for Machine Learning

Before you can use data for machine learning, it must be collected, cleaned, and prepared for analysis. This process is known as **data preprocessing**, and it involves several key steps to ensure the data is suitable for modeling.

1. **Data Collection**
   o Data can be collected from various sources, including:
      - **Databases**: Structured data can often be pulled from company databases using SQL queries.
      - **APIs**: Many modern applications and services offer APIs that allow you to collect data programmatically (e.g., Twitter API for tweets, Google Maps API for location data).
      - **Web Scraping**: Data from websites can be collected using tools like BeautifulSoup (for HTML data) or Scrapy (for web crawling).

- **Surveys and Forms**: For gathering data directly from users or customers, surveys or forms are often used.
- **Sensor Data**: In fields like healthcare, Internet of Things (IoT), and automotive, data is collected from various sensors (e.g., heart rate sensors, GPS).

2. **Data Cleaning** Once you have the data, it's essential to clean it to remove errors, inconsistencies, and unnecessary parts. Dirty data can lead to inaccurate models. Common cleaning tasks include:

   o **Handling Missing Data**: Missing values can be filled in with mean/median/mode imputation, or you may choose to remove rows or columns with excessive missing values.

   o **Removing Duplicates**: Duplicate data points can lead to biased results, so it's essential to identify and remove them.

   o **Correcting Inconsistencies**: Inconsistent data entries, such as different formats for dates or numbers, need to be standardized.

   o **Handling Outliers**: Outliers can skew model performance. Depending on the context, you might choose to remove outliers or transform them.

Example: If you're working with a dataset of people's ages and one of the ages is listed as 200, that's clearly an outlier and should be corrected or removed.

3. **Data Transformation** After cleaning the data, it's often necessary to transform it into a format suitable for machine learning algorithms.

   o **Feature Scaling**: Many machine learning models (like KNN, SVM, and neural networks) perform better when features have the same scale. Standardization (scaling features to have a mean of 0 and a standard deviation of 1) or normalization (scaling values to a [0,1] range) is often applied.

   o **Encoding Categorical Variables**: Machine learning algorithms typically require numerical data. Categorical data (e.g., "Male" or "Female") can be encoded using techniques like One-Hot Encoding or Label Encoding.

   o **Feature Engineering**: This involves creating new features from the existing data to improve model performance. For example, you might create a new feature for age ranges (e.g., 18-25, 26-35) from a continuous "age" column.

4. **Data Splitting**

   o Before training a model, you need to split your data into at least two sets:

- **Training Set**: Used to train the machine learning model.
- **Test Set**: Used to evaluate the performance of the model on unseen data.
  - Often, a third set, called a **validation set**, is used to fine-tune the model during training.
  - Typically, the data is split into a 70/30 or 80/20 ratio (training/testing).

Conclusion

Data is the core ingredient in machine learning, and understanding how to handle it is essential to building accurate models. This chapter introduced the importance of data, the different types of data (structured, unstructured, and semi-structured), and the essential steps in data collection and preprocessing. In the next chapters, you'll explore how to apply machine learning algorithms to this cleaned and preprocessed data to build predictive models.

CHAPTER 4

INTRODUCTION TO SUPERVISED LEARNING

Concept of Labels and Features

Supervised learning is one of the most fundamental approaches in machine learning. In supervised learning, a model is trained using a labeled dataset, meaning each input data point (or feature) is paired with a corresponding output value (or label). This training process allows the model to learn the relationship between the features and labels, and it can then predict the labels for new, unseen data.

1. **Features**

    o   Features, also known as input variables or predictors, are the attributes or characteristics of the data that are used to make predictions. These could be numerical (like age or income) or categorical (like gender or city).

    o   In machine learning, features are typically stored in columns of a dataset. For example, in a dataset predicting house prices, the features might include square footage, number of bedrooms, and location.

2. **Labels**

   o   Labels are the outcomes or target variables that the model aims to predict. In supervised learning, the labels are provided alongside the features during training.

   o   For example, in a classification task, the labels could be the categories to which the data belongs (e.g., "spam" or "not spam"). In a regression task, the labels could be continuous values, like the price of a house.

Example Dataset:

Square Footage	Bedrooms	Location	Price (Label)
1500	3	Suburban	$350,000
2000	4	Urban	$500,000
1200	2	Rural	$250,000

In this example, "Square Footage," "Bedrooms," and "Location" are the features, while "Price" is the label.

Regression vs Classification Problems

Supervised learning problems are typically divided into two main categories: **regression** and **classification**. The type of problem determines the kind of model you'll use and the format of your output (label).

1. **Regression Problems**
   o **Definition**: In regression, the goal is to predict a continuous output (real value) based on the given input features. This is commonly used in tasks like predicting house prices, stock market prices, or the temperature for the next day.
   o **Example**: Given the features of a house (e.g., square footage, number of bedrooms), predict its price. The label (price) is a continuous value.
   o **Output**: The output label is a real number (e.g., $350,000).
   o **Key Algorithms**:
      ▪ **Linear Regression**: A basic algorithm that models the relationship between features and labels by fitting a straight line to the data.
      ▪ **Decision Trees**: Can be used for both regression and classification problems.
      ▪ **Support Vector Machines (SVM)**: Can be used for regression tasks, called SVR (Support Vector Regression).

2. **Classification Problems**
   o **Definition**: In classification, the goal is to predict a discrete label or category based on the input

features. This is used in tasks like email spam detection, image classification, and medical diagnoses.

- o **Example**: Given the features of an email (e.g., subject, sender, content), classify whether it is spam or not. The label ("spam" or "not spam") is categorical.
- o **Output**: The output label is a category or class (e.g., "spam" or "not spam").
- o **Key Algorithms**:
  - **Logistic Regression**: Despite its name, logistic regression is primarily used for classification tasks.
  - **Decision Trees**: Used to classify data into different categories based on feature values.
  - **K-Nearest Neighbors (KNN)**: A classification algorithm based on the majority vote of nearest neighbors.

Common Algorithms in Supervised Learning

Supervised learning encompasses a wide range of algorithms, but two of the most fundamental ones are **Linear Regression** (used for regression problems) and **Logistic Regression** (used for classification problems). Let's take a closer look at these algorithms.

1. **Linear Regression**

   o **Purpose**: Linear regression is used for predicting a continuous numerical value based on one or more input features.

   o **How It Works**: The algorithm finds the best-fitting line (also known as the regression line) that minimizes the difference between the predicted values and the actual data points. This is done by minimizing the residual sum of squares (the difference between observed and predicted values).

   o **Equation**: The basic equation for a simple linear regression model is:

   $y=\beta_0+\beta_1 \cdot x$ y = \beta_0 + \beta_1 \cdot x $y=\beta_0+\beta_1 \cdot x$

   where:

   - yyy is the predicted value (label),
   - β_0\beta_0β_0 is the intercept,
   - β_1\beta_1β_1 is the coefficient of the feature xxx,
   - xxx is the feature.

   o **Example Use Case**: Predicting the price of a house based on its square footage.

   o **Key Features**:

- Assumes a linear relationship between the features and the target.
- Best used when there is a roughly linear relationship between the independent and dependent variables.

o **Code Example**:

```python
python

from sklearn.linear_model import LinearRegression
model = LinearRegression()
model.fit(X_train, y_train)
predictions = model.predict(X_test)
```

2. **Logistic Regression**

o **Purpose**: Despite its name, logistic regression is used for binary classification tasks, where the goal is to predict one of two possible classes (e.g., spam vs. not spam, disease vs. no disease).

o **How It Works**: Logistic regression uses a logistic (sigmoid) function to model the probability that a given input belongs to a certain class. The model outputs a probability between 0 and 1, and this probability is then mapped to one of the two classes (e.g., a probability greater than 0.5 might indicate the positive class).

o **Equation**: The logistic regression model can be represented as:

$$P(y=1|X) = \frac{1}{1 + e^{-(\beta_0 + \beta_1 \cdot x)}}$$

P(y=1|X)=11+e−(β0+β1·x)P(y=1|X) = \frac{1}{1 + e^{-(\beta_0 + \beta_1 \cdot x)}}P(y=1|X)=1+e−(β0+β1·x)1

where:

- $P(y=1|X)$ P(y=1|X)P(y=1|X) is the probability of the output being 1 (positive class),
- β_0 β0β0 is the intercept,
- β_1 β1β1 is the coefficient of the feature x xxx,
- e eee is the base of the natural logarithm.

o **Example Use Case**: Predicting whether an email is spam or not based on features like the subject line, sender, and body content.

o **Key Features**:
  - Suitable for binary classification problems.
  - Outputs probabilities, which can be interpreted as confidence in the classification.

o **Code Example**:

```python
python

from    sklearn.linear_model    import
LogisticRegression
model = LogisticRegression()
model.fit(X_train, y_train)
predictions = model.predict(X_test)
```

Conclusion

Supervised learning is a powerful and widely-used approach in machine learning. By understanding the key concepts of features and labels, and the differences between regression and classification problems, you're now ready to apply these techniques to real-world tasks. The linear regression and logistic regression algorithms are foundational, serving as the building blocks for many other complex models. In the following chapters, you will learn more about these algorithms and how to apply them to solve various machine learning problems.

CHAPTER 5

EXPLORING DATA WITH PYTHON

Data Loading, Exploration, and Visualization

Once you have your data, the next crucial step is to load, explore, and visualize it. These processes help you understand the structure and patterns within the data, identify potential issues (like missing values or outliers), and begin to formulate hypotheses for modeling.

1. **Data Loading**

    o   Python provides several libraries for loading data, with **Pandas** being the most popular for structured data (CSV, Excel, SQL, etc.). To load data into Python, you'll typically use the `pd.read_csv()` function for CSV files, or similar functions for other file formats.

    o   Example:

    ```python
    python

    import pandas as pd
    df = pd.read_csv('data.csv')  # Load
    a CSV file into a DataFrame
    ```

- o For other formats like Excel:

```python
df = pd.read_excel('data.xlsx')    #
Load data from an Excel file
```

- o For JSON or SQL databases, Pandas also offers functions like `read_json()` and `read_sql()`.

2. **Exploration**

- o After loading the data, the next step is to explore its structure and contents. This involves checking the first few rows, getting summary statistics, and identifying missing or inconsistent data.
- o Common functions for data exploration:
  - **df.head()**: Displays the first few rows of the dataset.

```python
print(df.head())    # Show the
first 5 rows of the data
```

  - **df.info()**: Provides a summary of the DataFrame, including column data types and non-null counts.

```python
```

```
df.info()  # Get the data types
and non-null values
```

- **df.describe()**: Generates summary statistics (mean, median, min, max, etc.) for numeric columns.

python

```
df.describe()  # Show summary
statistics    for    numerical
columns
```

- **df.columns**: List all column names.

python

```
print(df.columns)      #  List
column names
```

3. **Identifying Missing Data**

   o It's essential to check for missing values, which can lead to errors or bias in your machine learning models.

   o **Checking for missing values**:

python

```
df.isnull().sum()      #  Check  for
missing values in each column
```

- o **Handling missing values**: You can either drop rows with missing values or fill them using mean/median imputation, forward fill, or other strategies.

```python
df.fillna(df.mean(),   inplace=True)
# Fill missing values with the column
mean
```

Using Pandas for Data Manipulation

Pandas is a powerful library for data manipulation and is widely used in data science and machine learning tasks. It provides data structures like **DataFrame** and **Series**, which are excellent for working with structured data.

1. **Selecting Data**
   - o To select specific rows or columns in a DataFrame, you can use indexing and slicing techniques.
     - **Selecting columns**:

```python
```

```
df['column_name']  # Access a
single column as a Series
df[['col1', 'col2']]  # Access
multiple columns
```

- **Selecting rows by index**:

```python
df.iloc[0]  # Access the first
row by index
df.loc[0]   # Access a row by
its label (if labels are set)
```

2. **Filtering Data**
   o You can filter data based on conditions.

```python
df[df['Age'] > 30]   # Filter rows
where Age > 30
df[(df['Age'] > 30) & (df['Income']
> 50000)]  # Filter using multiple
conditions
```

3. **Grouping Data**
   o Pandas allows you to group data by specific columns and apply aggregation functions like sum(), mean(), and count() to gain insights.

48

```
python
```

```
df.groupby('Category')['Price'].mea
n()    # Group by 'Category' and
calculate the mean 'Price'
```

4. **Merging and Joining Data**

   o You can combine multiple DataFrames using
     `merge()`, which works similarly to SQL joins.

   ```
   python
   ```

   ```
   df1 = pd.read_csv('data1.csv')
   df2 = pd.read_csv('data2.csv')
   merged_df    =    pd.merge(df1,    df2,
   on='common_column', how='inner')    #
   Merge on a common column
   ```

5. **Sorting Data**

   o Sorting data is often necessary when you want to
     analyze the top or bottom entries.

   ```
   python
   ```

   ```
   df.sort_values(by='Price',
   ascending=False)    # Sort by 'Price'
   in descending order
   ```

Visualizing Data with Matplotlib and Seaborn

Data visualization is a critical step in understanding the patterns and relationships within your data. Python provides powerful libraries like **Matplotlib** and **Seaborn** for creating a wide range of static, animated, and interactive plots.

1. **Matplotlib Basics**

    o **Matplotlib** is a plotting library that allows you to create basic plots like line charts, bar charts, histograms, and more. It is highly customizable and works well for creating static visualizations.

    o Basic plotting with **Matplotlib**:

    python

```python
import matplotlib.pyplot as plt
plt.plot(df['x_column'],
df['y_column'])  # Line plot
plt.title('Plot Title')
plt.xlabel('X Axis Label')
plt.ylabel('Y Axis Label')
plt.show()  # Display the plot
```

    o **Scatter Plot** (useful for exploring relationships between two continuous variables):

    python

50

```
plt.scatter(df['x_column'],
df['y_column'])
plt.title('Scatter Plot')
plt.xlabel('X')
plt.ylabel('Y')
plt.show()
```

o **Histogram** (useful for understanding the distribution of a single variable):

python

```
plt.hist(df['column_name'], bins=10)
plt.title('Histogram')
plt.xlabel('Value')
plt.ylabel('Frequency')
plt.show()
```

2. **Seaborn for Enhanced Visualizations**

o **Seaborn** is built on top of Matplotlib and provides a high-level interface for drawing attractive and informative statistical graphics.

o **Seaborn** offers more advanced visualizations and is particularly useful for categorical data and statistical plots.

o **Example of a Box Plot** (useful for visualizing the distribution of a dataset and spotting outliers):

python

```
import seaborn as sns
sns.boxplot(x='Category', y='Price',
data=df)  # Box plot by 'Category'
plt.show()
```

o **Pairplot** (useful for visualizing relationships between multiple numerical variables):

python

```
sns.pairplot(df[['Age',   'Income',
'Price']])  # Pair plot of three
columns
plt.show()
```

o **Heatmap** (useful for visualizing correlation matrices or data tables):

python

```
correlation_matrix  =  df.corr()    #
Calculate the correlation matrix
sns.heatmap(correlation_matrix,
annot=True,  cmap='coolwarm')        #
Visualize correlation
plt.show()
```

3. **Customization of Plots**

- o Both **Matplotlib** and **Seaborn** allow you to customize the appearance of plots. You can change colors, labels, and titles, as well as add legends and grid lines.
- o Example:

```python
sns.barplot(x='Category', y='Price',
data=df, palette='Blues')
plt.title('Price by Category')
plt.xlabel('Category')
plt.ylabel('Price')
plt.show()
```

Conclusion

Exploring your data through loading, manipulation, and visualization is a crucial step in the machine learning workflow. In this chapter, we've learned how to load and explore data using **Pandas**, clean and manipulate it, and visualize it with **Matplotlib** and **Seaborn**. These skills form the foundation for understanding the patterns and trends in your data, which will guide the development of machine learning models in the subsequent chapters.

CHAPTER 6

PREPARING DATA FOR MACHINE LEARNING

Preparing your data is a crucial step in the machine learning pipeline. Raw data often contains errors, inconsistencies, or features that need to be transformed before it can be used to train machine learning models. In this chapter, we will focus on three key aspects of data preparation: **data cleaning**, **feature scaling and normalization**, and **encoding categorical variables**.

Data Cleaning (Handling Missing Values, Outliers)

Data cleaning is an essential step to ensure the quality of your dataset. In real-world datasets, you'll often encounter issues such as missing values, duplicate records, and outliers. These issues can significantly affect the performance of your machine learning models, so it's important to address them before moving forward.

1. **Handling Missing Values**
    o Missing values in your data can arise for several reasons, such as incomplete data collection, errors in data entry, or data loss during processing. Machine learning algorithms often

don't handle missing data well, so it's important to address these gaps.

Strategies to handle missing values:

o **Removing missing values**: If there are only a few missing values, you may choose to drop them from the dataset.

python

```python
df.dropna()    # Removes rows with missing values
```

o **Imputing missing values**: For numerical data, you can replace missing values with the mean, median, or mode. For categorical data, you can use the most frequent category (mode).

python

```python
df['column_name'].fillna(df['column_name'].mean(), inplace=True)    # Impute with mean
df['column_name'].fillna(df['column_name'].mode()[0], inplace=True)    # Impute with mode
```

- o **Forward/Backward fill**: For time-series data, you might choose to propagate the next or previous value.

python

```
df.fillna(method='ffill',
inplace=True)  # Forward fill missing
values
df.fillna(method='bfill',
inplace=True)     #  Backward  fill
missing values
```

2. **Handling Outliers**

- o Outliers are values that significantly differ from the other data points and can distort statistical analyses and model performance.
- o **Identifying outliers**: One common way to identify outliers is using **box plots** or **Z-scores**. A Z-score measures how many standard deviations away a data point is from the mean. A high Z-score (typically above 3 or below -3) indicates an outlier.

python

```
import numpy as np
from scipy import stats
```

56

```
z_scores                        =
np.abs(stats.zscore(df['column_name
']))
df = df[(z_scores < 3)]   # Remove
outliers based on Z-score
```

○ **Handling outliers**: You can either remove
   outliers or replace them with a value like the
   mean or median, depending on the context of the
   dataset.

```python
df['column_name']                        =
np.where(df['column_name']               >
upper_limit,            median_value,
df['column_name'])       #    Replace
outliers with median
```

Feature Scaling and Normalization

Feature scaling and normalization are essential when the range of values for different features varies widely. Some machine learning algorithms, such as K-Nearest Neighbors (KNN), Support Vector Machines (SVM), and gradient descent-based models (e.g., linear regression), are sensitive to the scale of the input features. Therefore, standardizing or normalizing the data can help improve model performance.

1. **Feature Scaling**

o Feature scaling involves rescaling the values of features so that they lie within a specific range. This ensures that no single feature dominates others due to its larger magnitude.

o **Standardization** (Z-score normalization): This method scales the data to have a mean of 0 and a standard deviation of 1.

python

```
from sklearn.preprocessing import
StandardScaler
scaler = StandardScaler()
df_scaled                          =
scaler.fit_transform(df[['feature1'
, 'feature2']])
```

Standardized formula:

$z=\frac{x-\mu}{\sigma}$z = \frac{x - \mu}{\sigma}$z=\frac{x-\mu}{\sigma}$

where:

- xxx is the original value,
- μ\mu$\mu$ is the mean,
- σ\sigma$\sigma$ is the standard deviation.

o **Min-Max Scaling**: This scales the data to a fixed range, typically [0, 1].

```python
from sklearn.preprocessing import
MinMaxScaler
scaler = MinMaxScaler()
df_scaled                        =
scaler.fit_transform(df[['feature1'
, 'feature2']])
```

Min-Max formula:

$$x_{scaled} = \frac{x - x_{min}}{x_{max} - x_{min}}$$

where:

- x_{min} is the minimum value in the feature,
- x_{max} is the maximum value.

2. **Normalization**

   o **Normalization** typically refers to rescaling the data so that the sum of squared values for each feature is 1 (unit vector).

   o This method is often used when the data needs to be transformed for specific algorithms like Neural Networks or clustering algorithms.

59

```
python
```

```
from sklearn.preprocessing import
Normalizer
normalizer = Normalizer()
df_normalized                      =
normalizer.fit_transform(df[['featu
re1', 'feature2']])
```

Encoding Categorical Variables

Machine learning models typically require numerical input, but real-world data often contains categorical features. Categorical data can represent various groups or classes, such as colors, product types, or locations. To use these features in a machine learning model, they must be encoded into numerical format.

1. **Label Encoding**
   o Label encoding assigns a unique integer to each category. For example, "red" might be encoded as 0, "blue" as 1, and "green" as 2.
   o While this method works for ordinal variables (where there is an inherent order), it may not be suitable for nominal variables, as it introduces an artificial order between the categories.

```
python
```

```
from    sklearn.preprocessing    import
LabelEncoder
encoder = LabelEncoder()
df['category_encoded']              =
encoder.fit_transform(df['category'
])
```

2. **One-Hot Encoding**

   o One-hot encoding creates new binary columns for each category in a categorical feature. Each column represents whether the observation belongs to a specific category (1 for yes, 0 for no).

   o This method is widely used for nominal variables, where no ordering is implied between categories.

   ```python
   python

   df_encoded                          =
   pd.get_dummies(df['category'],
   prefix='category')
   # Adds new columns for each category
   with binary values (0 or 1)
   ```

   o For example, if the 'Color' column has categories "red", "blue", and "green," one-hot encoding will create three new columns: `Color_red`, `Color_blue`, and `Color_green`.

3. **Ordinal Encoding**

- o For ordinal variables, where the categories have a natural order (e.g., "low," "medium," "high"), ordinal encoding assigns a numeric value based on the order.
- o Example:

```python
color_map = {'low': 0, 'medium': 1,
'high': 2}
df['color_encoded']              =
df['color'].map(color_map)
```

Conclusion

In this chapter, we covered essential techniques for preparing data for machine learning, focusing on data cleaning, feature scaling and normalization, and encoding categorical variables. Proper data preparation ensures that your dataset is in the best possible form for training machine learning models, which can significantly improve the performance and accuracy of your models. By handling missing values, outliers, scaling features, and encoding categorical variables, you're laying the foundation for building effective and reliable machine learning systems.

CHAPTER 7

LINEAR REGRESSION IN DETAIL

Understanding Linear Regression

Linear Regression is one of the simplest and most widely-used algorithms in machine learning. It is a **supervised learning** algorithm used for predicting a continuous target variable based on one or more input features. The core idea behind linear regression is to model the relationship between the input features and the target variable as a linear equation.

In simple terms, linear regression assumes that the relationship between the dependent variable y and the independent variable(s) X is linear. The goal of linear regression is to find the best-fit line (or hyperplane in higher dimensions) that minimizes the error between the predicted values and the actual values.

The Equation of Linear Regression: For a single feature (one independent variable), the linear regression equation is:

$$y = \beta_0 + \beta_1 \cdot X$$

where:

- y is the predicted value (target variable),

- XXX is the feature (independent variable),
- β0\beta_0β0 is the intercept (bias term),
- β1\beta_1β1 is the coefficient (weight) of the feature.

In the case of multiple features (multivariable linear regression), the equation extends to:

y=β0+β1·X1+β2·X2+···+βn·Xny = \beta_0 + \beta_1 \cdot X_1 + \beta_2 \cdot X_2 + \dots + \beta_n \cdot X_ny=β0+β1·X1+β2·X2 +···+βn·Xn

where:

- X1,X2,…,XnX_1, X_2, \dots, X_nX1,X2,…,Xn are the features (independent variables),
- β0\beta_0β0 is the intercept,
- β1,β2,…,βn\beta_1, \beta_2, \dots, \beta_nβ1,β2,…,βn are the coefficients of the features.

Key Concepts:

- **Intercept (β0\beta_0β0)**: The value of yyy when all features are zero.
- **Coefficients (β1,β2,…\beta_1, \beta_2, \dotsβ1,β2,…)**: These represent the change in the target variable for a unit change in the corresponding feature.

Linear regression tries to minimize the **residual sum of squares** (RSS), which is the sum of the squared differences between the actual values and the predicted values:

RSS=∑i=1n(yi−yi^)2RSS = \sum_{i=1}^{n} (y_i - \hat{y_i})^2RSS=i=1∑n(yi−yi^)2

where:

- yiy_iyi is the actual value,
- yi^\hat{y_i}yi^ is the predicted value.

Building Your First Machine Learning Model with Linear Regression

Now that we have a basic understanding of linear regression, let's walk through how to build your first machine learning model using this algorithm.

1. **Import Necessary Libraries**: To get started, we need to import libraries such as **Pandas** for data manipulation, **NumPy** for numerical operations, and **Scikit-learn** for implementing machine learning models.

   ```python
   import pandas as pd
   import numpy as np
   from sklearn.model_selection import train_test_split
   ```

```
from        sklearn.linear_model        import
LinearRegression
from          sklearn.metrics          import
mean_squared_error, r2_score
```

2. **Loading the Dataset**: Let's use a sample dataset for this example. For instance, we'll predict house prices based on square footage.

python

```
# Load the dataset
df = pd.read_csv('house_prices.csv')    #
Replace with your dataset's path
```

3. **Exploring and Preprocessing the Data**: Before training the model, it's important to check the data, clean it (handle missing values), and split it into features and target variables.

python

```
# Check the first few rows of the dataset
print(df.head())

# Handle missing values (if any)
df.fillna(df.mean(), inplace=True)      #
Impute missing values with the mean
```

```
# Split data into features (X) and target
variable (y)
X = df[['square_footage']]  # Independent
variable (feature)
y = df['price']  # Dependent variable
(target)
```

4. **Splitting the Data**: It's a good practice to split the data into training and test sets. Typically, 70-80% of the data is used for training, and the remaining 20-30% is used for testing.

python

```
# Split the data into training and testing
sets
X_train, X_test, y_train, y_test =
train_test_split(X, y, test_size=0.2,
random_state=42)
```

5. **Training the Model**: Now that we have our data, we can create a linear regression model and train it on the training data.

python

```
# Create a linear regression model
model = LinearRegression()
```

```
# Train the model
model.fit(X_train, y_train)
```

6. **Making Predictions**: After training the model, we can use it to predict house prices based on the test data.

```python
python
```

```
# Predict on the test data
y_pred = model.predict(X_test)
```

Evaluating the Model's Performance

Once the model has been trained and predictions have been made, the next step is to evaluate its performance. There are several metrics commonly used for evaluating linear regression models, including **Mean Squared Error (MSE)** and **R-squared (R2R^2R2)**.

1. **Mean Squared Error (MSE)**:
   o MSE measures the average squared difference between the predicted and actual values. A lower MSE indicates a better fit.
   o Formula for MSE:

   $$MSE=1n\sum i=1n(yi-yi^\wedge)2MSE = \frac{1}{n} \sum_{i=1}^{n} (y_i - \hat{y_i})^2MSE=n1 i=1\sum n(yi-yi^\wedge)2$$

2. python

3.

4. mse = mean_squared_error(y_test, y_pred)

5. print(f'Mean Squared Error: {mse}')

6. **R-squared (R2R^2R2)**:

   o The R2R^2R2 value indicates how well the model explains the variability of the target variable. It ranges from 0 to 1, with 1 indicating a perfect fit.

   o Formula for R2R^2R2:

   $$R2=1-\sum i=1n(yi-yi^)2\sum i=1n(yi-y^-)2R^2 = 1 - \frac{\sum_{i=1}^{n} (y_i - \hat{y_i})^2}{\sum_{i=1}^{n} (y_i - \bar{y})^2} R2=1-\sum i=1n(yi-y^-)2\sum i=1n(yi-yi^)2$$

7. where y¯\bar{y}y¯ is the mean of the actual values.

8. python

9.

10. r2 = r2_score(y_test, y_pred)

11. print(f'R-squared: {r2}')

12. **Visualizing the Results**: It's often helpful to visualize the model's performance by plotting the predictions against the actual values.

python

```python
import matplotlib.pyplot as plt

# Plot the actual vs predicted values
plt.scatter(X_test, y_test, color='blue',
label='Actual values')
plt.plot(X_test, y_pred, color='red',
label='Predicted values')
plt.title('Actual vs Predicted House
Prices')
plt.xlabel('Square Footage')
plt.ylabel('Price')
plt.legend()
plt.show()
```

Conclusion

Linear regression is a powerful and straightforward method for predicting continuous values. In this chapter, we learned the fundamentals of linear regression, built a simple model using **Scikit-learn**, and evaluated its performance using key metrics like **Mean Squared Error (MSE)** and **R-squared (R2R^2R2)**. Visualizing the results also provides a clear understanding of how well the model is performing.

Now that you have a solid understanding of linear regression, you're ready to apply this knowledge to more complex datasets and explore more advanced regression techniques. Linear regression forms the foundation for many machine learning tasks,

70

and mastering it will give you the skills to tackle a wide range of predictive modeling problems.

CHAPTER 8

CLASSIFICATION WITH LOGISTIC REGRESSION

Introduction to Classification

Classification is a type of supervised learning task where the goal is to predict a categorical outcome (also known as a class label) based on input features. Unlike regression, where the output is a continuous value, classification aims to assign each data point to a predefined category or class.

For example:

- **Email spam detection**: Classifying emails as either "spam" or "not spam."
- **Medical diagnosis**: Predicting whether a patient has a specific disease based on symptoms or test results (e.g., "disease" vs. "no disease").
- **Image classification**: Classifying images into categories such as "cat," "dog," "car," etc.

The objective in classification problems is to learn a model that can predict the class label of unseen data, given the features of that data.

There are various classification algorithms, and one of the most widely-used and simplest algorithms is **Logistic Regression**. Despite the name, logistic regression is actually a classification algorithm, not a regression algorithm. Let's dive deeper into how logistic regression works.

How Logistic Regression Works

Logistic regression is a linear model for binary classification, meaning it predicts one of two possible outcomes (0 or 1, true or false, yes or no). The model works by learning a relationship between the features and the probability of an instance belonging to one of the two classes.

1. **Sigmoid Function** The core of logistic regression is the **sigmoid function**, which maps any real-valued number (from negative to positive infinity) to a value between 0 and 1. This is useful for representing probabilities. The output of logistic regression is interpreted as the probability that a given data point belongs to the positive class (usually labeled as 1).

    The sigmoid function is defined as:

    $$\sigma(z) = \frac{1}{1 + e^{-z}}$$

    where:

o   zzz is the linear combination of the input features, similar to the output of linear regression:

$z=\beta_0+\beta_1 \cdot X_1+\beta_2 \cdot X_2+\dots+\beta_n \cdot X_n$z = \beta_0 + \beta_1 \cdot X_1 + \beta_2 \cdot X_2 + \dots + \beta_n \cdot X_nz=$\beta_0+\beta_1 \cdot X_1+\beta_2 \cdot X_2+\dots+\beta_n \cdot X_n$

o $\sigma(z)$\sigma(z)$\sigma(z)$ is the predicted probability that the observation belongs to class 1.

The output of the sigmoid function is interpreted as a probability. If $\sigma(z)$\sigma(z)$\sigma(z)$ is greater than or equal to 0.5, the instance is classified as class 1 (positive class); otherwise, it is classified as class 0 (negative class).

Example: If the logistic regression model predicts a probability of 0.7, the model would classify the instance as belonging to class 1 (positive class). If it predicts 0.3, the instance would belong to class 0 (negative class).

2. **Binary Classification with Logistic Regression** Logistic regression solves binary classification problems by calculating a probability that an observation belongs to class 1 based on its features and then applying a threshold to assign the final class label.

For example:

74

P(y=1|X)=11+e−(β0+β1·X)P(y=1|X) = \frac{1}{1 + e^{-(\beta_0 + \beta_1 \cdot X)}}P(y=1|X)=1+e−(β0+β1·X)1

where:

- ○ P(y=1|X)P(y=1|X)P(y=1|X) is the probability of class 1 given the input features XXX,
- ○ β0\beta_0β0 is the intercept, and β1\beta_1β1 is the coefficient for feature XXX.

3. **Multi-Class Classification** While logistic regression is primarily used for binary classification, it can also be extended to handle multiple classes (i.e., **multi-class classification**) through techniques like **One-vs-Rest (OvR)** or **Softmax regression**.

Building a Logistic Regression Model

Let's now walk through building a logistic regression model using Python. We will use the **Scikit-learn** library, which provides a simple implementation of logistic regression.

1. **Import Necessary Libraries**: First, we import the necessary libraries for data manipulation, machine learning, and evaluation.

```python
import pandas as pd
```

```
from      sklearn.model_selection      import
train_test_split
from      sklearn.linear_model      import
LogisticRegression
from       sklearn.metrics       import
confusion_matrix,       accuracy_score,
classification_report
```

2. **Loading the Dataset**: We'll use a simple example where we predict whether a person has a disease based on age and cholesterol levels.

python

```
# Load the dataset
df = pd.read_csv('health_data.csv')    #
Replace with your dataset's path

# Check the first few rows
print(df.head())
```

3. **Preparing the Data**: Let's split the data into features and target variable, and also split it into training and testing sets.

python

```
# Features (X) and target variable (y)
```

```
X = df[['age', 'cholesterol']]       #
Independent variables
y = df['disease']   # Dependent variable
(binary: 0 or 1)


# Split data into training and test sets
X_train, X_test, y_train, y_test =
train_test_split(X, y, test_size=0.2,
random_state=42)
```

4. **Training the Model**: Now, we create an instance of the **LogisticRegression** class and fit it to the training data.

python

```
# Create a logistic regression model
model = LogisticRegression()

# Train the model on the training data
model.fit(X_train, y_train)
```

5. **Making Predictions**: After training the model, we can use it to predict the target variable for the test data.

python

```
# Predict on the test data
y_pred = model.predict(X_test)
```

Evaluating a Logistic Regression Model

After building and training a logistic regression model, the next step is to evaluate its performance. Common metrics for evaluating classification models include **accuracy, confusion matrix, precision, recall**, and **F1-score**.

1. **Accuracy**: Accuracy is the proportion of correctly classified instances to the total instances.

   python

   ```python
   accuracy = accuracy_score(y_test, y_pred)
   print(f'Accuracy: {accuracy * 100:.2f}%')
   ```

2. **Confusion Matrix**: The confusion matrix shows the counts of true positives (TP), false positives (FP), true negatives (TN), and false negatives (FN). It helps to understand how well the model is classifying both classes.

   python

   ```python
   cm = confusion_matrix(y_test, y_pred)
   print('Confusion Matrix:')
   print(cm)
   ```

   The confusion matrix can be visualized using **Seaborn**:

   python

```
import seaborn as sns
import matplotlib.pyplot as plt
sns.heatmap(cm,    annot=True,    fmt='d',
cmap='Blues',  xticklabels=['No  Disease',
'Disease'],   yticklabels=['No   Disease',
'Disease'])
plt.xlabel('Predicted')
plt.ylabel('True')
plt.title('Confusion Matrix')
plt.show()
```

3. **Precision, Recall, and F1-Score**: These metrics provide more detailed insights into the performance of a classifier, especially when dealing with imbalanced datasets.

   o **Precision**: The ratio of correctly predicted positive observations to the total predicted positives:

   Precision=TPTP+FP\text{Precision} $=$ \frac{TP}{TP + FP}Precision=TP+FPTP

   o **Recall**: The ratio of correctly predicted positive observations to all observations in the actual class:

   Recall=TPTP+FN\text{Recall} = \frac{TP}{TP + FN}Recall=TP+FNTP

o **F1-Score**: The harmonic mean of precision and recall, providing a balance between the two:

F1-Score=2·Precision·RecallPrecision+Recall\text{F1-Score} = 2 \cdot \frac{\text{Precision} \cdot \text{Recall}}{\text{Precision} + \text{Recall}}F1-Score=2·Precision+RecallPrecision·Recall

4. These metrics can be obtained using the **classification_report** function from Scikit-learn:

5. python

6.

7. report = classification_report(y_test, y_pred)

8. print('Classification Report:')

9. print(report)

Conclusion

Logistic regression is a simple but powerful algorithm for binary classification tasks. In this chapter, we learned how logistic regression works, built a logistic regression model using **Scikit-learn**, and evaluated its performance using metrics like **accuracy, confusion matrix, precision, recall**, and **F1-score**.

With this foundation, you can apply logistic regression to various classification tasks, such as predicting customer churn, detecting fraud, or diagnosing diseases. The next step is to explore more advanced classification techniques and understand how to handle more complex problems with multiple classes or imbalanced datasets.

CHAPTER 9

K-NEAREST NEIGHBORS (KNN) ALGORITHM

Introduction to KNN

K-Nearest Neighbors (KNN) is a simple, intuitive, and versatile algorithm used for both **classification** and **regression** tasks. It is a **non-parametric** method, which means it makes no assumptions about the underlying data distribution. Instead, KNN works by comparing the distances between data points and using their proximity to make predictions.

KNN is often used in situations where the decision boundary between classes is highly non-linear, making it suitable for complex, real-world data. The algorithm is based on the principle of **locality**, meaning that the class or value of an instance is determined by the instances that are closest to it in the feature space.

In KNN:

- **K** refers to the number of nearest neighbors to consider when making a prediction.

- The algorithm calculates the **distance** (typically Euclidean distance) between the input data point and all other points in the training set.

- Based on the value of **K**, the algorithm then assigns the class or value of the majority (in classification) or the average (in regression) of the nearest neighbors.

Working with KNN for Classification and Regression

KNN can be used for both **classification** and **regression** tasks. Let's dive into how KNN works in each context:

1. **KNN for Classification**:
    o In classification tasks, the goal is to predict a **categorical** label (such as "spam" vs "not spam," or "disease" vs "no disease").
    o The KNN algorithm finds the K-nearest neighbors to a data point, then assigns the most frequent class among those neighbors as the predicted class.

Steps for KNN Classification:

   o **Step 1**: Choose a value for K (e.g., 3, 5, or 7). The value of K determines how many neighbors are considered.
   o **Step 2**: For a given data point, compute the distance between it and all other data points in the

dataset. Common distance metrics include **Euclidean distance**, **Manhattan distance**, or **Minkowski distance**.

- o **Step 3**: Identify the K-nearest neighbors (the K data points with the smallest distances).
- o **Step 4**: Assign the class label based on a majority vote from the K-nearest neighbors. The class that appears the most is assigned to the data point.

Example: If we have a dataset of patients with features like age and cholesterol levels, and the target is whether the patient has a disease (1 = disease, 0 = no disease), we can use KNN to predict whether a new patient has the disease based on their proximity to other patients in the dataset.

2. **KNN for Regression**:
   - o In regression tasks, the goal is to predict a **continuous** value (such as house price, salary, or temperature).
   - o Instead of voting on the most frequent class, KNN regression predicts the output value by averaging the values of the K-nearest neighbors.

Steps for KNN Regression:

- o **Step 1**: Choose a value for K.

- o **Step 2**: Calculate the distance between the data point to be predicted and all other data points in the dataset.
- o **Step 3**: Find the K-nearest neighbors.
- o **Step 4**: Predict the output value as the average of the output values of the K-nearest neighbors.

Example: In a dataset predicting house prices based on features like square footage and number of bedrooms, KNN regression would predict the price of a new house by averaging the prices of the K-nearest neighbors.

Working Example: KNN Classification

Let's walk through an example of using KNN for classification in Python. We will use the **Scikit-learn** library to implement KNN.

1. **Import Necessary Libraries**:

python

```
import pandas as pd
from     sklearn.model_selection     import
train_test_split
from        sklearn.neighbors        import
KNeighborsClassifier
from        sklearn.metrics        import
accuracy_score,        confusion_matrix,
classification_report
```

2. **Loading the Dataset**: For this example, let's assume we are using a simple dataset with two features: **age** and **cholesterol level**, and we want to classify whether a person has a disease (1 for "yes", 0 for "no").

python

```
# Load the dataset
df = pd.read_csv('health_data.csv')    #
Replace with your dataset's path

# Check the first few rows of the dataset
print(df.head())
```

3. **Preparing the Data**: We split the data into features (X) and the target variable (y), then split it into training and test sets.

python

```
# Features (X) and target variable (y)
X = df[['age', 'cholesterol']]    #
Independent variables
y = df['disease']   # Dependent variable
(binary: 0 or 1)

# Split data into training and test sets
(80% train, 20% test)
```

```
X_train,    X_test,    y_train,    y_test    =
train_test_split(X,    y,    test_size=0.2,
random_state=42)
```

4. **Training the Model**: We now create a KNN model and train it on the training data.

python

```
# Create a KNN classifier with K=3
model                                          =
KNeighborsClassifier(n_neighbors=3)

# Train the model on the training data
model.fit(X_train, y_train)
```

5. **Making Predictions**: After training the model, we can predict the target variable for the test set.

python

```
# Predict on the test data
y_pred = model.predict(X_test)
```

6. **Evaluating the Model**: We evaluate the model using metrics such as **accuracy**, **confusion matrix**, and **classification report**.

python

```
# Calculate the accuracy of the model
accuracy = accuracy_score(y_test, y_pred)
print(f'Accuracy: {accuracy * 100:.2f}%')


# Confusion matrix
cm = confusion_matrix(y_test, y_pred)
print('Confusion Matrix:')
print(cm)


# Classification report (precision,
recall, F1-score)
report = classification_report(y_test,
y_pred)
print('Classification Report:')
print(report)
```

Evaluating KNN Performance

To evaluate the performance of a KNN model, we use a variety of metrics, depending on the nature of the problem (binary classification, multi-class classification, or regression).

1. **Accuracy**: Accuracy measures the percentage of correctly classified instances. It is calculated as:

   Accuracy=Number of Correct PredictionsTotal Number of Predictions\text{Accuracy} = \frac{\text{Number of Correct Predictions}}{\text{Total Number of Predictions}}Accuracy=Total Number of PredictionsNumber of Correct Predictions

88

While accuracy is often used, it might not be the best metric when dealing with imbalanced datasets (where one class significantly outnumbers the other).

2. **Confusion Matrix**: The confusion matrix provides a detailed breakdown of the model's predictions, including:

   o **True Positives (TP)**: Correctly predicted positive cases.

   o **False Positives (FP)**: Incorrectly predicted positive cases.

   o **True Negatives (TN)**: Correctly predicted negative cases.

   o **False Negatives (FN)**: Incorrectly predicted negative cases.

Example output:

```lua
Confusion Matrix:
[[50 10]
 [ 5 35]]
```

This means the model correctly predicted 50 instances as "no disease" and 35 instances as "disease." It incorrectly predicted 10 "no disease" instances as "disease" and 5 "disease" instances as "no disease."

3. **Precision, Recall, and F1-Score**:

   o **Precision**: The percentage of correct positive predictions among all positive predictions. Precision is important when the cost of false positives is high.

   o **Recall**: The percentage of correct positive predictions among all actual positives. Recall is important when the cost of false negatives is high.

   o **F1-Score**: The harmonic mean of precision and recall, providing a balance between the two.

4. **K-Value Selection**: The choice of **K** can significantly affect the performance of the KNN model. A smaller K (e.g., 1 or 3) might lead to overfitting, where the model captures noise in the data, while a larger K might smooth out the decision boundary too much and underfit the data. It's important to experiment with different values of K to find the optimal one for your dataset.

You can use cross-validation techniques, such as **GridSearchCV**, to automatically select the best K-value.

python

```
from    sklearn.model_selection    import
GridSearchCV

param_grid = {'n_neighbors': [1, 3, 5, 7,
9, 11]}
```

```
grid_search                              =
GridSearchCV(KNeighborsClassifier(),
param_grid, cv=5)
grid_search.fit(X_train, y_train)

print(f'Best                          K:
{grid_search.best_params_["n_neighbors"]}
')
```

Conclusion

K-Nearest Neighbors (KNN) is a simple and effective algorithm for classification and regression tasks. In this chapter, we learned how KNN works by considering the distance between data points, how to build a KNN model using **Scikit-learn**, and how to evaluate its performance using metrics such as **accuracy**, **confusion matrix**, and **precision/recall/F1-score**.

The performance of the KNN model depends heavily on the choice of K and the distance metric used, making it important to experiment with different parameters for optimal results. KNN is particularly useful for problems where the decision boundaries are highly non-linear, and it can handle both classification and regression tasks with minimal parameter tuning.

CHAPTER 10

DECISION TREES AND RANDOM FORESTS

Understanding Decision Trees

A **Decision Tree** is a popular and intuitive machine learning algorithm used for both **classification** and **regression** tasks. It works by recursively splitting the data into subsets based on the feature that provides the best separation of the target variable. Each split creates a decision node, which tests a feature, and the leaves of the tree represent the predicted output.

The goal of a decision tree is to split the dataset into homogeneous groups where the target variable is as pure as possible. A decision tree is structured like a flowchart where:

- **Nodes** represent the features of the data.
- **Branches** represent the outcomes of the decision (splits based on feature values).
- **Leaves** represent the final predicted outcomes or class labels.

Key Concepts:

- **Root Node**: The first decision node that represents the entire dataset. It is the starting point for the decision-making process.
- **Splits/Branches**: The process of dividing the dataset based on a feature value.
- **Leaf Node**: The final output of the decision process, representing the class or value to be predicted.
- **Gini Impurity** and **Entropy** are commonly used metrics to determine the best feature to split the data.

1. **Gini Impurity**: Measures the purity of the node. The lower the Gini Impurity, the better the feature split.

Gini=1−∑i=1kpi2Gini = 1 - \sum_{i=1}^{k} p_i^2Gini=1−i=1∑kpi2

where pip_ipi is the probability of each class in the node.

2. **Entropy**: Measures the disorder or uncertainty in the node. The goal is to minimize entropy.

Entropy=−∑i=1kpilog⁣2(pi)Entropy = -\sum_{i=1}^{k} p_i \log_2(p_i)Entropy=−i=1∑kpilog2(pi)

where pip_ipi is the probability of each class in the node.

The algorithm selects the feature that best reduces the impurity (or entropy) and recursively splits the dataset until a stopping criterion is met, such as a maximum depth, minimum samples in a node, or when further splitting doesn't improve the model.

Implementing Decision Trees for Classification

Let's walk through an example of how to implement a **Decision Tree** for classification using **Scikit-learn**.

1. **Import Necessary Libraries**: We'll use **Pandas** for data manipulation, **Scikit-learn** for implementing the Decision Tree, and **Matplotlib** for visualization.

   ```python
   python

   import pandas as pd
   from sklearn.model_selection import train_test_split
   from sklearn.tree import DecisionTreeClassifier, plot_tree
   from sklearn.metrics import accuracy_score, classification_report, confusion_matrix
   ```

2. **Loading and Preparing the Dataset**: We will use a dataset for binary classification, such as predicting whether a person has a disease based on age and cholesterol levels.

```
python
```

```python
# Load the dataset
df = pd.read_csv('health_data.csv')    #
Replace with your dataset's path

# Check the first few rows of the dataset
print(df.head())

# Split the data into features (X) and
target variable (y)
X = df[['age', 'cholesterol']]    #
Independent variables
y = df['disease']   # Dependent variable
(binary: 0 or 1)

# Split the data into training and testing
sets (80% train, 20% test)
X_train, X_test, y_train, y_test =
train_test_split(X, y, test_size=0.2,
random_state=42)
```

3. **Training the Decision Tree Model**: We can create a **DecisionTreeClassifier** and train it on the training data.

```
python
```

```python
# Create a Decision Tree classifier
```

```
model                                    =
DecisionTreeClassifier(criterion='gini',
max_depth=5, random_state=42)


# Train the model
model.fit(X_train, y_train)
```

4. **Making Predictions**: After training the model, we can predict the class labels on the test set.

```python
# Predict on the test data
y_pred = model.predict(X_test)
```

5. **Evaluating the Model**: We can use metrics like **accuracy**, **confusion matrix**, and **classification report** to evaluate the performance of the model.

```python
# Calculate accuracy
accuracy = accuracy_score(y_test, y_pred)
print(f'Accuracy: {accuracy * 100:.2f}%')

# Confusion Matrix
cm = confusion_matrix(y_test, y_pred)
print('Confusion Matrix:')
print(cm)
```

```
# Classification Report
report   =   classification_report(y_test,
y_pred)
print('Classification Report:')
print(report)
```

6. **Visualizing the Decision Tree**: One of the advantages of decision trees is their interpretability. We can visualize the tree to see how the model makes its decisions.

python

```
# Plot the decision tree
plot_tree(model,              filled=True,
feature_names=['age',      'cholesterol'],
class_names=['No Disease', 'Disease'])
```

Improving Performance with Random Forests

While decision trees are easy to interpret, they are prone to overfitting, especially when the tree grows too deep. Overfitting occurs when the model becomes too complex and starts capturing noise in the data rather than the underlying patterns, which results in poor generalization to new data.

Random Forests are an ensemble learning method that improves the performance of decision trees by aggregating predictions from multiple decision trees, each trained on a different subset of the data. The primary idea behind random forests is to reduce overfitting and increase the model's robustness.

1. **How Random Forests Work**:
   - o **Bootstrap Sampling**: Random forests use **bootstrap sampling** to create different training subsets by randomly sampling with replacement from the original dataset. Each tree is trained on a different random sample of the data.
   - o **Random Feature Selection**: During the construction of each tree, instead of considering all features for each split, random forests select a random subset of features at each decision node. This helps reduce correlation between trees and makes the model more robust.
   - o **Ensemble Learning**: After the trees are trained, the random forest aggregates their predictions. For classification, the majority vote of all trees is used; for regression, the average of all trees is used.

2. **Implementing Random Forests**: We can easily implement **Random Forests** using **Scikit-learn**.

```python
from sklearn.ensemble import RandomForestClassifier
```

```python
# Create a Random Forest classifier
rf_model                             =
RandomForestClassifier(n_estimators=100,
random_state=42)

# Train the model
rf_model.fit(X_train, y_train)

# Predict on the test data
y_pred_rf = rf_model.predict(X_test)

# Evaluate the Random Forest model
accuracy_rf    =    accuracy_score(y_test,
y_pred_rf)
print(f'Random        Forest        Accuracy:
{accuracy_rf * 100:.2f}%')

# Confusion Matrix
cm_rf      =      confusion_matrix(y_test,
y_pred_rf)
print('Random Forest Confusion Matrix:')
print(cm_rf)

# Classification Report
report_rf = classification_report(y_test,
y_pred_rf)
print('Random      Forest      Classification
Report:')
```

```
print(report_rf)
```

3. **Advantages of Random Forests**:
   o **Reduced Overfitting**: By averaging the predictions of many decision trees, random forests are less likely to overfit compared to individual decision trees.
   o **Improved Accuracy**: Random forests often outperform individual decision trees because they aggregate the knowledge from multiple trees, making the model more stable and accurate.
   o **Feature Importance**: Random forests can also help identify which features are the most important in making predictions, which can be useful for feature selection.

4. **Visualizing Random Forests**: While visualizing an individual decision tree is easy, visualizing the entire random forest can be challenging due to the large number of trees. However, we can assess feature importance:

```
python
```

```
# Plot feature importance
import matplotlib.pyplot as plt
feature_importance              =
rf_model.feature_importances_
plt.bar(['age',           'cholesterol'],
feature_importance)
```

```
plt.title('Feature Importance')
plt.show()
```

Conclusion

In this chapter, we explored the **Decision Tree** algorithm and learned how to implement it for classification tasks using **Scikit-learn**. We also discussed how decision trees can be prone to overfitting, and how **Random Forests** improve upon decision trees by aggregating multiple trees and reducing overfitting through **bootstrap sampling** and **random feature selection**.

Random forests are a powerful ensemble method that often yields better performance than a single decision tree, especially for complex datasets. They are robust, accurate, and provide valuable insights into feature importance, making them a go-to choice for many machine learning tasks.

CHAPTER 11

INTRODUCTION TO NEURAL NETWORKS

What is a Neural Network?

A **Neural Network** is a type of machine learning model inspired by the structure and function of the human brain. It is composed of layers of interconnected nodes, known as **neurons**, which work together to process input data, recognize patterns, and make predictions or decisions. Neural networks are especially powerful for tasks such as image recognition, speech processing, and natural language understanding.

The fundamental idea behind a neural network is that it can learn complex patterns by adjusting the weights of connections between neurons during training. Neural networks are often used for **deep learning** tasks, where they are called **Deep Neural Networks (DNNs)**. These models are capable of handling large datasets and performing well in high-dimensional spaces, which makes them particularly useful for complex problems.

Key Characteristics of Neural Networks:

- **Non-linearity**: Neural networks are able to model non-linear relationships between input and output data, making them more flexible than linear models.

- **Learning through Backpropagation**: Neural networks use a method called **backpropagation** to adjust the weights of neurons in response to the error in the network's output.

- **Layered Structure**: Neural networks consist of multiple layers of neurons, each of which learns different levels of abstraction in the data.

Neural networks are the foundation of deep learning techniques, where networks with many layers (called **deep networks**) can model highly complex relationships. They are widely used in areas such as computer vision, speech recognition, and language translation.

Basic Structure of a Neural Network

A neural network consists of several components that work together to process data and make predictions. The main components include **neurons, layers**, and **activation functions**.

1. **Neurons (Artificial Neurons)**:
   o A neuron in a neural network is a computational unit that receives inputs, processes them, and produces an output.

- o Each neuron is connected to other neurons through **weights**, which determine the strength of the connection between neurons. Each connection also has an associated **bias** that allows the model to shift the output of the neuron.

The output of a neuron is calculated by applying a mathematical function (usually involving a weighted sum of the inputs and a bias). The formula for a neuron's output is:

Output=f(∑i=1nwixi+b)\text{Output} = f\left(\sum_{i=1}^{n} w_i x_i + b \right)Output=f(i=1∑nwixi +b)

where:

- o wiw_iwi is the weight of the input xix_ixi,
- o bbb is the bias,
- o fff is the activation function.

2. **Layers**: Neural networks are organized into layers of neurons:

- o **Input Layer**: This layer receives the input data. Each neuron in the input layer represents one feature of the data.
- o **Hidden Layers**: These are intermediate layers between the input and output. A neural network

104

can have one or more hidden layers. Each hidden layer transforms the input data into more abstract representations. The more hidden layers, the deeper the network.

- o **Output Layer**: This layer produces the final output or prediction of the model. For classification tasks, the output layer might have one neuron for each possible class (with one-hot encoding used to represent the classes).

A simple feedforward neural network can consist of just an input layer, one hidden layer, and an output layer.

3. **Activation Functions**: An activation function is a mathematical function applied to the output of each neuron. It introduces **non-linearity** into the model, allowing it to learn complex patterns in the data.

Some commonly used activation functions include:

- o **Sigmoid**: Outputs values between 0 and 1, often used for binary classification tasks.

  σ(x)=11+e−x\sigma(x) = \frac{1}{1 + e^{-x}}σ(x)=1+e−x1

- o **ReLU (Rectified Linear Unit)**: Outputs the input if it's positive, or zero if it's negative. It's widely used in hidden layers because of its ability to speed up training and avoid vanishing gradients.

$$\text{ReLU}(x) = \max(0, x)$$

o **Softmax**: Used in the output layer for multi-class classification tasks. It outputs a probability distribution over multiple classes.

$$\text{Softmax}(x_i) = \frac{e^{x_i}}{\sum_{j} e^{x_j}}$$

o **Tanh (Hyperbolic Tangent)**: Outputs values between -1 and 1, and is used in many older networks.

$$\tanh(x) = \frac{e^{x} - e^{-x}}{e^{x} + e^{-x}}$$

The choice of activation function depends on the problem and the specific characteristics of the data.

Building a Simple Neural Network with Python

Now that we have a basic understanding of neural networks, let's walk through how to build a simple neural network for classification using Python and **Keras**, a high-level deep learning library that runs on top of **TensorFlow**.

1. **Import Necessary Libraries**: We need to install **TensorFlow** (which includes Keras) and import the required libraries.

```bash
bash
```

```python
pip install tensorflow
python

import numpy as np
import pandas as pd
from tensorflow.keras.models import Sequential
from tensorflow.keras.layers import Dense
from sklearn.model_selection import train_test_split
from sklearn.preprocessing import StandardScaler
```

2. **Loading and Preparing the Dataset**: Let's assume we're using a simple dataset with two features, such as

predicting whether a person has a disease based on their age and cholesterol levels.

```python
# Load the dataset
df = pd.read_csv('health_data.csv')   # Replace with your dataset's path

# Features and target variable
X = df[['age', 'cholesterol']]   # Independent variables
y = df['disease']   # Dependent variable (binary: 0 or 1)

# Split the data into training and testing sets
X_train, X_test, y_train, y_test = train_test_split(X, y, test_size=0.2, random_state=42)

# Standardize the features (important for neural networks)
scaler = StandardScaler()
X_train = scaler.fit_transform(X_train)
X_test = scaler.transform(X_test)
```

3. **Building the Neural Network**: Now, we can define a simple feedforward neural network. We will create a

model using the **Sequential** class, which allows us to stack layers of neurons.

```python
python

# Create a neural network model
model = Sequential()

# Input layer (we define it as the first hidden layer)
model.add(Dense(8,          input_dim=2,
activation='relu'))    # 8 neurons, ReLU
activation

# Hidden layer
model.add(Dense(4, activation='relu'))    #
4 neurons, ReLU activation

# Output layer (sigmoid activation for binary classification)
model.add(Dense(1, activation='sigmoid'))
# Output layer with 1 neuron

# Compile the model
model.compile(loss='binary_crossentropy',
optimizer='adam', metrics=['accuracy'])
```

4. **Training the Model**: After defining the model, we can train it on the training data.

```
python
```

```
# Train the model
model.fit(X_train, y_train, epochs=50,
batch_size=10, verbose=1)
```

5. **Evaluating the Model**: Once the model is trained, we can evaluate its performance on the test data.

```
python
```

```
# Evaluate the model
loss, accuracy = model.evaluate(X_test,
y_test)
print(f'Accuracy: {accuracy * 100:.2f}%')
```

6. **Making Predictions**: After training, we can use the model to make predictions on new data.

```
python
```

```
# Make predictions
predictions = model.predict(X_test)
predictions = (predictions > 0.5) #
Convert probabilities to binary
predictions
```

Conclusion

Neural networks are a powerful tool in machine learning, capable of modeling complex patterns in data. In this chapter, we explored the basic structure of neural networks, including neurons, layers, and activation functions. We also walked through building a simple neural network for binary classification using Python and Keras.

Neural networks, especially deep neural networks, are capable of solving a wide range of problems, including those that are too complex for traditional algorithms. The flexibility of neural networks comes at a cost of more computational power and training time, but the results often justify the investment, especially for complex tasks like image recognition, speech processing, and natural language understanding.

CHAPTER 12

DEEP LEARNING AND CONVOLUTIONAL NEURAL NETWORKS (CNNS)

Overview of Deep Learning

Deep Learning is a subset of machine learning that focuses on using multi-layered neural networks to model complex patterns and representations in data. It is particularly well-suited for tasks involving high-dimensional data, such as images, audio, and text. Deep learning models, often referred to as **deep neural networks**, contain multiple layers that allow them to automatically extract features and learn hierarchical patterns from raw data.

Deep learning has revolutionized fields like computer vision, natural language processing, and speech recognition. Unlike traditional machine learning algorithms, deep learning models do not require manual feature extraction. Instead, they can learn directly from raw data and automatically discover the important features needed for classification, prediction, and other tasks.

Key characteristics of deep learning:

- **Hierarchical Feature Learning**: Deep learning models learn increasingly abstract features as data passes through each layer. For example, in image classification, early layers may detect simple edges, while deeper layers may recognize shapes, objects, or scenes.

- **End-to-End Learning**: Deep learning models are capable of learning from raw data (e.g., images, audio, or text) directly to output predictions, eliminating the need for manual feature engineering.

- **Large-Scale Data**: Deep learning models typically require large amounts of labeled data for training, as well as significant computational resources.

Deep learning models often utilize GPUs (Graphics Processing Units) and specialized hardware to process large amounts of data efficiently. Frameworks like **TensorFlow**, **Keras**, and **PyTorch** have made it easier to build and train deep learning models, significantly reducing the complexity of working with neural networks.

Introduction to Convolutional Neural Networks (CNNs)

Convolutional Neural Networks (CNNs) are a class of deep learning models that are particularly well-suited for analyzing and processing visual data, such as images and videos. CNNs are designed to automatically and adaptively learn spatial hierarchies of features from input images, making them the most effective models for image-related tasks such as image classification, object detection, and image segmentation.

The key components of a CNN are **convolutional layers, pooling layers**, and **fully connected layers**. Each of these components plays a vital role in processing and learning from image data:

1. **Convolutional Layers**:
   o The convolutional layer is the core building block of a CNN. It applies a convolution operation to the input image using a set of learnable filters (also known as kernels). Each filter detects specific features in the image, such as edges, textures, or colors.
   o The convolution operation involves sliding a filter across the image and computing a weighted sum of the pixel values in the region the filter is covering. The result of the convolution is a feature map that highlights the presence of certain features in the image.
   o Multiple filters are applied in parallel, each detecting different features, resulting in several feature maps.
2. **Activation Function (ReLU)**:
   o After convolution, an activation function is applied, typically the **ReLU (Rectified Linear Unit)** function. ReLU introduces non-linearity to

the model, allowing it to learn complex patterns in the data.

ReLU(x)=max⁡[fo](0,x)\text{ReLU}(x)   =   \max(0, x)ReLU(x)=max(0,x)

3. **Pooling Layers**:

   o Pooling layers are used to downsample the feature maps, reducing their spatial dimensions while retaining important information. The most common pooling operation is **max pooling**, which takes the maximum value from each region of the feature map.

   o Pooling helps reduce the computational load and prevent overfitting by summarizing features.

4. **Fully Connected Layers**:

   o After several convolutional and pooling layers, the high-level features extracted by the network are passed through fully connected layers. These layers are similar to the layers in traditional neural networks, where each neuron is connected to all the neurons in the previous layer.

   o The final fully connected layer produces the output of the network, which is typically a vector of class probabilities in the case of classification tasks.

5. **Softmax**:

o The **Softmax** activation function is used in the output layer of a CNN for multi-class classification problems. It converts the raw output of the network into probabilities, where each class is represented by a probability value between 0 and 1, and the sum of all probabilities is equal to 1.

Building a Simple Image Classification Model

In this section, we will build a simple image classification model using CNNs with **Keras** (which runs on top of **TensorFlow**). We'll use the **MNIST** dataset, a collection of 28x28 grayscale images of handwritten digits (0-9), which is commonly used to demonstrate image classification tasks.

1. **Import Necessary Libraries**: First, we need to import the required libraries.

python

```
import numpy as np
import tensorflow as tf
from    tensorflow.keras    import    layers,
models
from    tensorflow.keras.datasets    import
mnist
```

```
from      tensorflow.keras.utils      import
to_categorical
```

2. **Loading and Preparing the Dataset**: Keras provides easy access to the MNIST dataset. We will load the data, normalize the images, and convert the labels to one-hot encoded format.

python

```
# Load the MNIST dataset
(X_train,  y_train),  (X_test,  y_test)  =
mnist.load_data()

# Reshape  the  images  to  have  a  single
channel (grayscale)
X_train                                   =
X_train.reshape((X_train.shape[0], 28, 28,
1))
X_test = X_test.reshape((X_test.shape[0],
28, 28, 1))

# Normalize pixel values  to  be  between  0
and 1
X_train, X_test = X_train / 255.0, X_test
/ 255.0

# Convert labels to one-hot encoded format
y_train = to_categorical(y_train, 10)
```

117

```
y_test = to_categorical(y_test, 10)
```

3. **Building the CNN Model**: We'll create a simple CNN architecture with 2 convolutional layers followed by max pooling, a fully connected layer, and an output layer.

python

```python
# Create the CNN model
model = models.Sequential()

# Convolutional layer 1
model.add(layers.Conv2D(32,      (3,      3),
activation='relu',   input_shape=(28,   28,
1)))

# Pooling layer 1
model.add(layers.MaxPooling2D((2, 2)))

# Convolutional layer 2
model.add(layers.Conv2D(64,      (3,      3),
activation='relu'))

# Pooling layer 2
model.add(layers.MaxPooling2D((2, 2)))

# Flatten the 2D feature maps into 1D
model.add(layers.Flatten())
```

```
# Fully connected layer
model.add(layers.Dense(128,
activation='relu'))


# Output layer with softmax activation for
multi-class classification
model.add(layers.Dense(10,
activation='softmax'))
```

4. **Compiling the Model**: After defining the model, we need to compile it by specifying the loss function, optimizer, and evaluation metrics.

python

```
# Compile the model
model.compile(optimizer='adam',

loss='categorical_crossentropy',
                metrics=['accuracy'])
```

5. **Training the Model**: Now, we can train the model on the training data.

python

```
# Train the model
model.fit(X_train,    y_train,    epochs=5,
batch_size=64,    validation_data=(X_test,
y_test))
```

119

6. **Evaluating the Model**: After training, we evaluate the model's performance on the test set.

python

```
# Evaluate the model on the test data
test_loss,            test_acc            =
model.evaluate(X_test, y_test, verbose=2)
print(f"Test accuracy: {test_acc}")
```

7. **Making Predictions**: Finally, we can use the trained model to make predictions on new data.

python

```
# Predict the class of the first test image
prediction = model.predict(X_test[:1])
print(f"Predicted                class:
{np.argmax(prediction)}")
```

Conclusion

In this chapter, we explored **Deep Learning** and **Convolutional Neural Networks (CNNs)**, which have become the go-to models for image-related tasks such as image classification and object detection. We learned the basic structure of a CNN, including convolutional layers, pooling layers, activation functions, and the importance of deep learning for feature extraction.

We also built a simple image classification model using the **MNIST dataset** with **Keras**. This example demonstrates how CNNs can automatically learn spatial hierarchies of features from raw image data, making them highly effective for computer vision tasks.

CNNs are widely used in a variety of applications, including self-driving cars, facial recognition, and medical imaging, due to their ability to automatically learn complex patterns and make accurate predictions. As you continue to work with deep learning, you can explore more advanced architectures, such as **ResNet**, **Inception**, and **VGG**, which have been designed to improve performance in even more complex tasks.

CHAPTER 13

MODEL EVALUATION TECHNIQUES

Overfitting vs Underfitting

When building machine learning models, one of the key challenges is ensuring that the model generalizes well to unseen data. Two common problems that can arise during model training are **overfitting** and **underfitting**.

1. **Overfitting**:
   - **Definition**: Overfitting occurs when a model learns not only the underlying patterns in the training data but also the noise or random fluctuations. This leads to a model that is too complex and performs well on the training data but poorly on unseen data (test data).
   - **Symptoms**: A model that shows high accuracy on the training set but low accuracy on the test set is likely overfitting.
   - **Cause**: Overfitting is often caused by having too many features, too complex a model (e.g., deep neural networks with many layers), or not enough training data.

- o **Solution**: To avoid overfitting, you can:
  - Simplify the model (e.g., reduce the number of features or use a less complex algorithm).
  - Use **regularization techniques** (like L1 or L2 regularization) to penalize large coefficients.
  - Increase the size of the training data to provide a better representation of the problem.
  - Use **early stopping** when training models like neural networks.
  - Employ **cross-validation** (discussed below) to tune the model's hyperparameters and prevent overfitting.

2. **Underfitting**:
   - o **Definition**: Underfitting occurs when a model is too simple to capture the underlying patterns in the data. The model makes incorrect assumptions about the data and performs poorly on both the training and test sets.
   - o **Symptoms**: A model that has poor performance on both the training set and the test set is likely underfitting.
   - o **Cause**: Underfitting is typically caused by using too simple a model, such as linear regression on

data that requires a more complex model (e.g., neural networks or decision trees).

- o **Solution**: To avoid underfitting, you can:
  - Use a more complex model (e.g., decision trees, random forests, or neural networks).
  - Include more relevant features in the model.
  - Allow the model to train for longer or use more sophisticated algorithms.

Balancing Overfitting and Underfitting: The goal is to find the **right balance** between overfitting and underfitting. A model that generalizes well to unseen data will perform well in both training and testing phases. Techniques like **cross-validation** and **regularization** can help in finding this balance.

Cross-Validation Methods

Cross-validation is a technique used to assess how well a machine learning model generalizes to unseen data. It involves splitting the dataset into multiple subsets (or folds) and training the model on different subsets while testing it on the remaining data. Cross-validation helps provide a more reliable estimate of model performance and reduces the risk of overfitting or underfitting.

1. **K-Fold Cross-Validation**:

   o **Definition**: K-fold cross-validation involves splitting the dataset into **K** equally-sized folds. The model is trained on $K-1$ folds and tested on the remaining fold. This process is repeated K times, with each fold being used as the test set once.

   o **Steps**:

      ▪ Split the dataset into K equal-sized subsets.

      ▪ For each subset, train the model on the remaining $K-1$ subsets and test it on the current subset.

      ▪ Calculate the performance metric (e.g., accuracy, precision) for each fold.

      ▪ Average the results of all K tests to get a final performance estimate.

   o **Example**: If you use 5-fold cross-validation (K=5), the dataset is divided into 5 subsets. The model is trained 5 times, each time using 4 subsets for training and 1 subset for testing.

   o **Benefits**: Cross-validation reduces the variability of the performance estimate by averaging over multiple folds, which leads to more reliable results than using a single train-test split.

2. **Stratified K-Fold Cross-Validation**:

- o **Definition**: In **Stratified K-Fold Cross-Validation**, each fold contains approximately the same proportion of each class as the original dataset. This is especially important for imbalanced datasets, where one class is significantly more frequent than the other(s).

- o **Benefit**: Stratified K-fold ensures that each fold is a good representative of the overall class distribution, which is crucial when working with imbalanced data.

3. **Leave-One-Out Cross-Validation (LOO-CV):**

- o **Definition**: In **Leave-One-Out Cross-Validation**, each data point is used once as a test set, while the remaining data points are used for training. This means that if you have NNN data points, the model will be trained NNN times.

- o **Benefit**: LOO-CV uses all of the data for both training and testing, but it is computationally expensive for large datasets.

Performance Metrics

After training a machine learning model, it is essential to evaluate its performance to determine how well it generalizes to new, unseen data. Common performance metrics for classification models include **accuracy**, **precision**, **recall**, **F1-score**, and **ROC**

curve. Each metric provides a different perspective on model performance.

1. **Accuracy**:
   o **Definition**: Accuracy measures the proportion of correctly predicted instances out of all instances.

   Accuracy=Number of Correct PredictionsTotal Number of Predictions\text{Accuracy} = \frac{\text{Number of Correct Predictions}}{\text{Total Number of Predictions}}Accuracy=Total Number of PredictionsNumber of Correct Predictions

   o **Limitations**: Accuracy is not always a good metric, especially for imbalanced datasets, where the model could achieve high accuracy by simply predicting the majority class.

2. **Precision**:
   o **Definition**: Precision measures the proportion of true positive predictions out of all predicted positives.

   Precision=TPTP+FP\text{Precision} = \frac{TP}{TP + FP}Precision=TP+FPTP

   o **When to Use**: Precision is particularly important when the cost of false positives is high (e.g., fraud detection, medical diagnoses).

3. **Recall (Sensitivity):**

   o **Definition**: Recall measures the proportion of true positive predictions out of all actual positives.

   $$\text{Recall} = \frac{TP}{TP + FN}$$

   o **When to Use**: Recall is important when the cost of false negatives is high (e.g., disease detection, where missing a positive case can be critical).

4. **F1-Score**:

   o **Definition**: The F1-score is the harmonic mean of precision and recall. It balances the trade-off between precision and recall.

   $$\text{F1-score} = 2 \cdot \frac{\text{Precision} \cdot \text{Recall}}{\text{Precision} + \text{Recall}}$$

   o **When to Use**: The F1-score is particularly useful when you need to balance both precision and recall, especially in imbalanced datasets.

5. **ROC Curve (Receiver Operating Characteristic Curve):**

o **Definition**: The ROC curve is a graphical representation of a model's performance at different classification thresholds. It plots the **True Positive Rate (TPR)** or **Recall** on the y-axis and the **False Positive Rate (FPR)** on the x-axis.

o **Area Under the Curve (AUC)**: The **AUC** is a summary statistic for the ROC curve. It represents the likelihood that the model ranks a randomly chosen positive instance higher than a randomly chosen negative instance. AUC ranges from 0 to 1, where 1 indicates perfect classification and 0.5 indicates a random classifier.

o **When to Use**: ROC curves are useful for evaluating binary classifiers, especially when dealing with imbalanced classes. A higher AUC generally indicates better model performance.

Example of Plotting ROC Curve:

python

```
from sklearn.metrics import roc_curve, auc
import matplotlib.pyplot as plt

fpr, tpr, thresholds = roc_curve(y_test,
y_pred_prob)
```

```
roc_auc = auc(fpr, tpr)

plt.figure()
plt.plot(fpr,   tpr,   color='darkorange',
lw=2, label='ROC curve (area = %0.2f)' %
roc_auc)
plt.plot([0,   1],   [0,   1],   color='navy',
lw=2, linestyle='--')
plt.xlim([0.0, 1.0])
plt.ylim([0.0, 1.05])
plt.xlabel('False Positive Rate')
plt.ylabel('True Positive Rate')
plt.title('Receiver            Operating
Characteristic (ROC) Curve')
plt.legend(loc="lower right")
plt.show()
```

Conclusion

In this chapter, we discussed key **model evaluation techniques** such as overfitting vs underfitting, cross-validation methods, and performance metrics like accuracy, precision, recall, F1-score, and the ROC curve.

Understanding these evaluation methods is crucial for assessing the generalization ability of a model and making improvements as needed. Cross-validation techniques help us ensure that our models are not overfitting or underfitting, while performance metrics provide deeper insights into model performance, especially in cases where accuracy alone may not be sufficient.

By using these techniques, you can build robust models that perform well on unseen data and deliver reliable results in real-world applications.

CHAPTER 14

INTRODUCTION TO UNSUPERVISED LEARNING

What is Unsupervised Learning?

Unsupervised learning is a type of machine learning where the model is trained on data without labeled outcomes (i.e., there are no predefined categories or labels for the target variable). Unlike supervised learning, where we have input-output pairs to guide the model's learning process, unsupervised learning focuses on finding hidden patterns, relationships, or structures in the data.

The key difference in unsupervised learning is that the algorithm must **discover patterns or groupings** in the data by itself. Unsupervised learning is particularly useful for tasks where labeled data is not available, or when the goal is to explore the underlying structure of the data.

Two common types of unsupervised learning problems are **clustering** and **association**:

- **Clustering** involves grouping data points into similar clusters based on their features.

- **Association** involves finding interesting relationships or patterns among variables in the data (often used for market basket analysis).

Clustering vs Association Problems

1. **Clustering Problems**:
   - **Definition**: Clustering is the task of grouping similar data points together. The goal is to partition the dataset into subsets or **clusters**, where data points within each cluster are more similar to each other than to data points in other clusters.
   - **Example**: A common use case for clustering is customer segmentation in marketing, where customers are grouped into clusters based on their purchasing behavior, so that each group can be targeted with specific marketing strategies.
   - **Key Characteristics**:
     - The number of clusters is often not known beforehand.
     - Data points are assigned to one of the clusters, and the clustering process should minimize the variance within each cluster.

- Unsupervised clustering can be used for exploratory data analysis to find inherent groupings in data.

2. **Association Problems**:

   o **Definition**: Association learning is used to identify interesting relationships or patterns between variables in large datasets. It's often used in market basket analysis, where we want to find associations between products purchased together.

   o **Example**: In a retail setting, association rules might reveal that customers who buy bread are likely to also buy butter. These relationships are expressed in the form of **association rules** (e.g., "If a customer buys bread, they are likely to also buy butter").

   o **Key Characteristics**:

     - Association rules typically consist of **antecedents** (e.g., "bread") and **consequents** (e.g., "butter").

     - Common measures for evaluating association rules include **support**, **confidence**, and **lift**:

       - **Support**: The proportion of transactions that contain both the antecedent and consequent.

- **Confidence**: The probability that the consequent occurs given the antecedent.
- **Lift**: The ratio of the observed support to the expected support if the items were independent.

Common Algorithms: K-Means, DBSCAN

Several algorithms are used in unsupervised learning, and two of the most popular for clustering tasks are **K-Means** and **DBSCAN**.

1. **K-Means Clustering**:
    o **Definition**: K-Means is one of the simplest and most widely-used clustering algorithms. The goal of K-Means is to partition the data into K distinct, non-overlapping clusters.
    o **How it works**:
        - First, you specify the number of clusters **K**.
        - The algorithm starts by randomly selecting **K** centroids (the center points of each cluster).
        - Each data point is then assigned to the nearest centroid.

135

- After all data points have been assigned to clusters, the centroids are recalculated as the mean of all points in each cluster.
- The process of assigning points to the nearest centroid and updating centroids repeats until convergence (i.e., the centroids no longer change).

o **Pros**:

- Easy to understand and implement.
- Works well for well-separated clusters.

o **Cons**:

- The number of clusters **K** must be specified in advance, and the algorithm may not perform well if the clusters have irregular shapes or different densities.
- Sensitive to initial centroid positions and outliers.

o **Example** (Using **Scikit-learn**):

```python
python


from sklearn.cluster import KMeans
import matplotlib.pyplot as plt

# Assume X is your dataset (e.g.,
customer data)
kmeans = KMeans(n_clusters=3)
kmeans.fit(X)
```

136

```
# Get the cluster centers and labels
centers = kmeans.cluster_centers_
labels = kmeans.labels_

# Plot the clusters
plt.scatter(X[:,    0],    X[:,    1],
c=labels, cmap='viridis')
plt.scatter(centers[:,           0],
centers[:,    1],    s=300,    c='red',
marker='x')   # Mark centroids
plt.show()
```

2. **DBSCAN (Density-Based Spatial Clustering of Applications with Noise)**:

   o **Definition**: DBSCAN is a density-based clustering algorithm that groups together closely packed points while marking points in low-density regions as outliers.

   o **How it works**:

      ▪ The algorithm defines clusters based on **density** rather than distance. It starts with a random point and checks if it has enough neighboring points within a given radius. If so, it forms a cluster.

      ▪ The algorithm is able to find clusters of arbitrary shapes, unlike K-Means, which assumes spherical clusters.

137

- DBSCAN also has the advantage of identifying outliers as points that do not belong to any cluster.

o **Key Parameters**:

- **Epsilon (ε)**: The maximum distance between two points to be considered neighbors.

- **MinPts**: The minimum number of points required to form a dense region (a cluster).

o **Pros**:

- Can find clusters of arbitrary shapes.

- Does not require the number of clusters to be specified in advance.

- Can detect outliers (noise points).

o **Cons**:

- Sensitive to the choice of parameters (Epsilon and MinPts).

- Struggles with data of varying density, where some clusters are much denser than others.

o **Example** (Using **Scikit-learn**):

```python

from sklearn.cluster import DBSCAN
import matplotlib.pyplot as plt
```

```
# Assume X is your dataset (e.g.,
customer data)
db = DBSCAN(eps=0.3, min_samples=10)
labels = db.fit_predict(X)

# Plot the clusters
plt.scatter(X[:,    0],    X[:,    1],
c=labels, cmap='viridis')
plt.show()
```

Choosing Between K-Means and DBSCAN

1. **K-Means** works well when:
   - The number of clusters is known in advance.
   - The data consists of well-separated, spherical clusters.
   - You don't need to worry about outliers in your data.

2. **DBSCAN** works well when:
   - You don't know the number of clusters and need the algorithm to figure it out.
   - The data has clusters of arbitrary shapes.
   - You need the ability to detect outliers or noise points.

Conclusion

Unsupervised learning is a powerful tool for exploring data and finding hidden patterns when labeled data is not available. In this chapter, we discussed the key concepts in unsupervised learning, including the difference between **clustering** and **association** problems. We then explored two popular clustering algorithms: **K-Means**, which is simple and effective for well-separated clusters, and **DBSCAN**, which can handle clusters of arbitrary shape and outliers.

Choosing the right algorithm depends on the nature of the data and the problem at hand. While K-Means is efficient and easy to implement, DBSCAN provides more flexibility in terms of handling irregular shapes and detecting outliers. Unsupervised learning continues to be a key approach for discovering patterns in large, unlabeled datasets.

CHAPTER 15

K-MEANS CLUSTERING

How K-Means Clustering Works

K-Means Clustering is one of the most widely used unsupervised learning algorithms for **partitioning** a dataset into distinct clusters. The objective of K-Means is to partition the data into KKK clusters, where each data point belongs to the cluster with the closest centroid. The centroid is the mean of all points in the cluster and represents the "center" of that cluster.

The algorithm follows these basic steps:

1. **Initialization**:
   - Choose KKK initial centroids (this can be done randomly or using more advanced methods like the **K-Means++** initialization).

2. **Assigning Data Points to Clusters**:
   - For each data point, calculate its distance from each centroid (usually using **Euclidean distance**).
   - Assign each data point to the cluster whose centroid is the closest.

3. **Updating Centroids**:

o After all data points have been assigned to clusters, recalculate the centroids by taking the mean of all points in each cluster.

4. **Repeat**:

   o Repeat steps 2 and 3 until the centroids no longer change (or the change is smaller than a predefined threshold). This indicates that the algorithm has converged and the clusters are stable.

Mathematical Formula for Euclidean Distance: For each data point $(x1,x2,\dots,xn)(x\_1, x\_2, \dots, x\_n)(x1,x2,\dots,xn)$, and each centroid $(c1,c2,\dots,cn)(c\_1, c\_2, \dots, c\_n)(c1,c2,\dots,cn)$, the Euclidean distance is given by:

$$d=\sum i=1n(xi-ci)2d = \sqrt{\sum_{i=1}^{n} (x\_i - c\_i)^2}d=i=1\sum n(xi-ci)2$$

Where xix_ixi is a feature value from the data point and cic_ici is the corresponding feature value from the centroid.

Key Parameters:

- KKK: The number of clusters to form.
- **Centroid**: The central point of each cluster, calculated as the mean of the points in the cluster.

Implementing K-Means in Python

To implement **K-Means clustering** in Python, we can use the **Scikit-learn** library, which provides an easy-to-use implementation of the K-Means algorithm. Below is a step-by-step guide to implementing K-Means on a simple dataset.

1. **Import Libraries**: Start by importing the necessary libraries for data manipulation, clustering, and visualization.

   python

   ```python
   import numpy as np
   import pandas as pd
   from sklearn.cluster import KMeans
   from sklearn.datasets import make_blobs
   import matplotlib.pyplot as plt
   ```

2. **Generating a Sample Dataset**: For this example, we will generate a simple 2D dataset using `make_blobs` that consists of three clusters.

   python

   ```python
   # Generate synthetic dataset with 3
   clusters
   ```

```
X,    y    =    make_blobs(n_samples=300,
centers=3,                cluster_std=0.60,
random_state=0)


# Visualize the dataset
plt.scatter(X[:,  0],  X[:,  1],  s=30,
cmap='viridis')
plt.title("Generated Data Points")
plt.show()
```

3. **Fitting K-Means Model**: Now we will apply the K-Means algorithm to the dataset to identify the clusters.

```
python


# Create a KMeans model with K=3 (3
clusters)
kmeans = KMeans(n_clusters=3)


# Fit the model to the data
kmeans.fit(X)


# Get the centroids of the clusters
centroids = kmeans.cluster_centers_


# Get the labels (i.e., which cluster each
data point belongs to)
labels = kmeans.labels_


# Visualize the results
```

```
plt.scatter(X[:, 0], X[:, 1], c=labels,
s=30, cmap='viridis')
plt.scatter(centroids[:, 0], centroids[:,
1], c='red', s=200, marker='X')      #
Centroids
plt.title("Clusters and Centroids")
plt.show()
```

4. **Choosing the Optimal Number of Clusters (K)**: One important aspect of K-Means is selecting the right number of clusters KKK. We can do this using the **Elbow Method**, which plots the **inertia** (sum of squared distances from each point to its assigned cluster centroid) for different values of KKK. The point where the inertia starts to level off is considered the optimal KKK.

python

```
# Calculate inertia for different values of
K
inertia = []
for k in range(1, 11):
    kmeans = KMeans(n_clusters=k)
    kmeans.fit(X)
    inertia.append(kmeans.inertia_)

# Plot the Elbow graph
plt.plot(range(1,      11),      inertia,
marker='o')
```

```
plt.title("Elbow Method")
plt.xlabel('Number of Clusters (K)')
plt.ylabel('Inertia')
plt.show()
```

The **elbow point** is where the inertia starts to decrease at a slower rate, indicating the ideal number of clusters.

5. **Predicting New Data Points**: After training the model, you can use it to predict the cluster for new, unseen data points:

python

```
new_data = np.array([[2, 4], [1, 2]])    #
New data points
predictions = kmeans.predict(new_data)
print("Predicted clusters:", predictions)
```

Evaluating K-Means Performance

Evaluating the performance of K-Means clustering is a bit different from evaluating supervised learning models, as there is no "ground truth" to compare the results to. However, we can still use several methods to assess the quality of the clustering:

1. **Inertia (Sum of Squared Errors)**:
   o   Inertia is the sum of squared distances between each data point and its assigned centroid. A lower

inertia means that the clusters are more compact and better separated.

```python
# Calculate inertia
inertia = kmeans.inertia_
print("Inertia (sum of squared errors):",
inertia)
```

2. **Silhouette Score**:

   o The **Silhouette Score** is a measure of how similar each point is to its own cluster compared to other clusters. It ranges from -1 to 1:
     - A value closer to 1 indicates that points are well-clustered.
     - A value close to 0 indicates that points are on or near the decision boundary between clusters.
     - A value closer to -1 indicates that points may have been assigned to the wrong cluster.

```python
from        sklearn.metrics        import
silhouette_score
```

```
# Calculate silhouette score
score = silhouette_score(X, labels)
print("Silhouette Score:", score)
```

3. **Visualizing the Clusters**:

   o   Visualizing the data with cluster labels can give a good understanding of how well the algorithm has clustered the data. If the clusters are clearly separated in the plot, the algorithm has done well.

   o   You can also visualize clusters in higher-dimensional data using **Dimensionality Reduction** techniques like **PCA** or **t-SNE**.

Conclusion

In this chapter, we covered the **K-Means Clustering** algorithm, a powerful technique for partitioning data into distinct clusters. We walked through the steps of how K-Means works, from initializing centroids to assigning data points to clusters and updating the centroids iteratively. We also demonstrated how to implement K-Means in Python using **Scikit-learn**, visualize the clusters, and use the **Elbow Method** and **Silhouette Score** to evaluate the clustering performance.

While K-Means is effective for many clustering tasks, it is important to note that it works best when the clusters are well-separated and spherical. For more complex or irregular data,

148

algorithms like **DBSCAN** (Density-Based Spatial Clustering) may be more suitable.

With the foundation of K-Means clustering, you can now apply this algorithm to a variety of unsupervised learning tasks and explore data-driven insights from complex datasets.

CHAPTER 16

DIMENSIONALITY REDUCTION WITH PCA

Introduction to Principal Component Analysis (PCA)

Principal Component Analysis (PCA) is a powerful technique used in **unsupervised learning** to reduce the dimensionality of a dataset while retaining as much variability (information) as possible. The goal of PCA is to simplify complex datasets with many features into a smaller set of features, called **principal components**, that still capture the essential patterns in the data.

PCA works by transforming the data into a new set of orthogonal axes called **principal components**, which are ordered in such a way that the first few components capture the most variance in the data. Each principal component is a linear combination of the original features, and these components are chosen to maximize the variance in the data.

Key benefits of PCA:

- **Dimensionality reduction**: PCA reduces the number of features in a dataset while preserving most of the variance.

- **Visualization**: PCA can be used to reduce high-dimensional data to two or three dimensions for visualization purposes.
- **Noise reduction**: By removing less significant dimensions (those with low variance), PCA helps to reduce noise and improve the performance of machine learning algorithms.

Mathematical Concepts in PCA:

- PCA involves the following mathematical steps:
    1. **Centering**: Subtract the mean of each feature from the data (to ensure the data is centered around the origin).
    2. **Covariance Matrix**: Calculate the covariance matrix, which captures the relationships between the features.
    3. **Eigenvalues and Eigenvectors**: The principal components are the eigenvectors of the covariance matrix, and the eigenvalues represent the amount of variance captured by each principal component.
    4. **Projection**: The data is projected onto the new principal component axes to reduce the dimensionality.

The number of principal components chosen depends on the amount of variance you want to retain from the original data. You can often capture most of the variance with just a few components.

Using PCA for Feature Reduction

Dimensionality reduction via PCA is particularly useful when:

- **The dataset has many features**, and you want to reduce the complexity of the model while maintaining important patterns in the data.
- **High-dimensional data is sparse** and contains redundant or highly correlated features.
- **Data visualization** is required, and you need to reduce the data to two or three dimensions to visualize the relationships between data points.

Steps for Using PCA for Feature Reduction:

1. **Standardize the data**: PCA is sensitive to the scale of the data, so it's important to standardize the features (e.g., by using **StandardScaler** in Scikit-learn) so that each feature has zero mean and unit variance.
2. **Fit the PCA model**: Fit PCA to the standardized data and choose the number of components based on how much variance you want to retain.

3. **Transform the data**: Use the fitted PCA model to transform the original data into a new set of features (principal components).

4. **Analyze the components**: Examine the explained variance ratio of each component to understand how much information each principal component retains from the original data.

Explained Variance:

- **Explained variance** tells you how much variance each principal component explains in the data. You can plot the **cumulative explained variance** to decide how many components are needed to capture most of the information.

Implementing PCA in Python

Let's walk through an example of applying PCA for feature reduction using **Scikit-learn**.

1. **Import Libraries**: We need to import **PCA** from **Scikit-learn** and other necessary libraries.

```python
python

import numpy as np
import pandas as pd
```

```
from sklearn.decomposition import PCA
from      sklearn.preprocessing      import
StandardScaler
from sklearn.datasets import load_iris
import matplotlib.pyplot as plt
```

2. **Load and Prepare the Dataset**: For this example, we will use the **Iris dataset**, which contains 150 samples of iris flowers with 4 features (sepal length, sepal width, petal length, and petal width).

python

```
# Load the Iris dataset
data = load_iris()
X = data.data  # Feature matrix
y = data.target  # Target labels
```

3. **Standardize the Data**: PCA is sensitive to the scales of the data, so we need to standardize it to have zero mean and unit variance.

python

```
scaler = StandardScaler()
X_scaled = scaler.fit_transform(X)
```

4. **Fit PCA**: Now, we can fit PCA to the scaled data. Let's start by reducing the data to 2 components (for visualization purposes).

python

```
# Apply PCA to reduce the data to 2
components
pca = PCA(n_components=2)
X_pca = pca.fit_transform(X_scaled)


# Print the explained variance ratio for
each component
print(f"Explained variance ratio for each
component:
{pca.explained_variance_ratio_}")
print(f"Total      explained      variance:
{sum(pca.explained_variance_ratio_)}")
```

The explained variance ratio tells you how much of the total variance is explained by each of the two principal components. This is helpful for understanding how well the reduced data represents the original data.

5. **Visualizing the Results**: After reducing the data to 2 dimensions, we can visualize the data points in a 2D plot. We will color the points based on their class labels to see how well PCA has separated the data.

python

```python
# Plot the PCA-transformed data
plt.figure(figsize=(8, 6))
plt.scatter(X_pca[:, 0], X_pca[:, 1], c=y,
cmap='viridis')
plt.xlabel('Principal Component 1')
plt.ylabel('Principal Component 2')
plt.title('PCA of Iris Dataset')
plt.colorbar(label='Target Class')
plt.show()
```

The scatter plot shows how the data points are distributed in the reduced 2D space, with different colors representing different iris species.

6. **Choosing the Number of Components**: To decide how many principal components to use, you can plot the **cumulative explained variance** and select the number of components that capture most of the variance (e.g., 95%).

python

```python
# Plot cumulative explained variance
plt.figure(figsize=(8, 6))
plt.plot(range(1,
len(pca.explained_variance_ratio_) + 1),
np.cumsum(pca.explained_variance_ratio_),
marker='o')
```

156

```
plt.xlabel('Number of Components')
plt.ylabel('Cumulative          Explained
Variance')
plt.title('Cumulative  Explained  Variance
vs Number of Components')
plt.show()
```

This plot helps you determine how many components are necessary to capture a certain percentage of the total variance in the data.

Conclusion

In this chapter, we explored **Principal Component Analysis (PCA)**, a technique used for **dimensionality reduction** and **feature extraction**. PCA allows you to reduce the number of features in a dataset while preserving as much information as possible. This is particularly useful in high-dimensional datasets, where reducing the number of features can improve model performance and simplify data visualization.

We walked through the steps of implementing PCA in Python using **Scikit-learn**, including:

- Standardizing the data,
- Fitting PCA and reducing the dimensionality,
- Visualizing the transformed data, and

- Evaluating the explained variance to determine how many components are needed.

PCA is a powerful tool for many machine learning tasks, especially when dealing with high-dimensional data. By applying PCA, you can reduce complexity, improve model performance, and gain better insights into your data.

CHAPTER 17

INTRODUCTION TO NATURAL LANGUAGE PROCESSING (NLP)

What is NLP?

Natural Language Processing (NLP) is a field of artificial intelligence (AI) that focuses on the interaction between computers and human (natural) languages. The goal of NLP is to enable machines to understand, interpret, and generate human language in a way that is meaningful and useful.

NLP involves several tasks, such as:

- **Text classification**: Categorizing text into predefined categories (e.g., spam detection, sentiment analysis).
- **Named entity recognition (NER)**: Identifying and classifying entities such as names, dates, and locations within text.
- **Language translation**: Automatically translating text from one language to another.
- **Speech recognition**: Converting spoken language into text.
- **Text generation**: Generating human-like text based on certain input or context (e.g., chatbots, language models).

NLP combines linguistics (the study of language) with computer science and machine learning techniques to process and understand text data. It is used in a wide range of applications, including search engines, virtual assistants, sentiment analysis, and more.

Challenges in NLP:

- **Ambiguity**: Human language is often ambiguous, with multiple meanings for the same word or sentence depending on context.
- **Context**: The meaning of words often depends on the surrounding words or previous sentences.
- **Variety of languages**: Different languages have different structures and rules, making it difficult to create universal NLP systems.

Basic Text Processing (Tokenization, Lemmatization)

Before applying machine learning models or performing deeper analysis, text data typically undergoes preprocessing to transform raw text into a format suitable for analysis. Some key preprocessing tasks in NLP include **tokenization**, **lemmatization**, and other methods like stopword removal and stemming.

1. **Tokenization**:
   o **Definition**: Tokenization is the process of splitting text into smaller units, called **tokens**.

Tokens can be words, sentences, or even subwords. Tokenization is often the first step in text processing, as it breaks down the text into manageable pieces.

- o **Types of Tokenization**:
  - **Word Tokenization**: Splitting a sentence into individual words. For example:
    - Text: "Natural Language Processing is amazing!"
    - Tokens: ["Natural", "Language", "Processing", "is", "amazing", "!"]
  - **Sentence Tokenization**: Splitting a large document into individual sentences.
- o **Example using Python's NLTK (Natural Language Toolkit)**:

```python
import nltk
from      nltk.tokenize      import
word_tokenize

text = "Natural Language Processing
is amazing!"
tokens = word_tokenize(text)
print(tokens)
```

Output:

```css
['Natural',          'Language',
'Processing', 'is', 'amazing', '!']
```

2. **Lemmatization**:

   o **Definition**: Lemmatization is the process of reducing a word to its base or root form (called a **lemma**). Unlike **stemming**, which simply removes prefixes or suffixes to reduce words to their stems (often resulting in non-dictionary forms), lemmatization considers the meaning of the word and its context to return a valid word form.

   o For example:
      - "running" becomes "run"
      - "better" becomes "good"
      - "cats" becomes "cat"

   o **Why Lemmatization is Important**: Lemmatization ensures that words with similar meanings are treated as the same word, improving the quality of analysis and predictions.

   o **Example using Python's NLTK**:

```python
```

```
from          nltk.stem          import
WordNetLemmatizer

lemmatizer = WordNetLemmatizer()
print(lemmatizer.lemmatize("running
", pos="v"))  # Verb lemmatization
print(lemmatizer.lemmatize("better"
,   pos="a"))            #    Adjective
lemmatization
```

Output:

```
arduino

run
good
```

- o In the example above, the word "running" is reduced to its base form "run", and "better" is reduced to "good".

3. **Stopword Removal**:

- o **Definition**: Stopwords are common words (such as "is", "the", "and", "in", etc.) that are often removed from text during preprocessing, as they do not carry significant meaning for most NLP tasks.
- o **Example using NLTK**:

```
python
```

163

```
from nltk.corpus import stopwords

stop_words                    =
set(stopwords.words('english'))
filtered_tokens = [word for word in
tokens    if    word.lower()    not    in
stop_words]
print(filtered_tokens)
```

o **Example output**:

```css
css
```

```
['Natural',              'Language',
'Processing', 'amazing', '!']
```

Real-World Examples of NLP Applications

NLP is widely used in real-world applications to solve a variety of problems. Some of the most common and impactful applications of NLP include:

1. **Sentiment Analysis**:
   - o **Definition**: Sentiment analysis involves determining the sentiment or opinion expressed in a piece of text, such as a product review, tweet, or social media post. It can be classified as positive, negative, or neutral.

- Example: A company might use sentiment analysis to analyze customer feedback and determine the overall sentiment about their products.

- **Example using Python**:

```python
from textblob import TextBlob

text = "I love this product, it's amazing!"
blob = TextBlob(text)
print(blob.sentiment)    # Outputs polarity and subjectivity
```

2. **Machine Translation**:
   - **Definition**: Machine translation uses NLP techniques to automatically translate text from one language to another. Google Translate, DeepL, and other similar services use machine translation to break down language barriers.
   - **Example**: Automatically translating product descriptions on e-commerce websites for international customers.

3. **Chatbots and Virtual Assistants**:
   - **Definition**: NLP is a key component of **chatbots** and **virtual assistants** (like Siri, Alexa, and

Google Assistant). These systems understand and process natural language commands, respond with appropriate actions, and help users with a variety of tasks (e.g., setting reminders, playing music, answering questions).

o **Example**: A virtual assistant interpreting the phrase "What's the weather like today?" and providing the weather forecast.

4. **Named Entity Recognition (NER)**:

o **Definition**: NER is a task in NLP where the goal is to identify and classify named entities (e.g., person names, locations, dates) in a piece of text.

o **Example**: Identifying names of people and organizations in news articles or legal documents.

o **Example using Python's spaCy**:

```python

import spacy
nlp = spacy.load("en_core_web_sm")

text = "Apple is looking to buy a startup in San Francisco for $1 billion."
doc = nlp(text)

for ent in doc.ents:
    print(ent.text, ent.label_)
```

o **Example output**:

```
nginx

Apple ORG
San Francisco GPE
$1 billion MONEY
```

5. **Text Summarization**:

   o **Definition**: Text summarization is the process of creating a shortened version of a long document while retaining its essential meaning. This can be done in two ways:

   - **Extractive Summarization**: Extracting key sentences from the original document.

   - **Abstractive Summarization**: Generating new sentences that convey the same meaning as the original text.

   o **Example**: Summarizing long articles or research papers to give users quick insights.

6. **Text Generation**:

   o **Definition**: Text generation involves creating new content based on existing input. Models like **GPT-3** (Generative Pretrained Transformer 3) are capable of generating coherent and contextually relevant text based on a given prompt.

o **Example**: Writing articles, generating poetry, or completing sentences in a conversational agent.

o **Example using OpenAI's GPT-3 API**:

```python
import openai
openai.api_key = 'your-api-key'

prompt = "Once upon a time in a land far, far away,"
response = openai.Completion.create(
    engine="text-davinci-003",
    prompt=prompt,
    max_tokens=50
)

print(response.choices[0].text.strip())
```

Conclusion

In this chapter, we introduced **Natural Language Processing (NLP)**, a powerful subfield of AI that focuses on enabling machines to understand and process human language. We covered key concepts like **tokenization, lemmatization**, and stopword removal, which are essential for preprocessing text data.

NLP has a wide range of real-world applications, from **sentiment analysis** to **machine translation** and **chatbots**. With the advent of advanced models like GPT-3, NLP continues to evolve, enabling machines to generate, understand, and interact with human language in ways that were once considered impossible.

As you continue exploring NLP, the field offers many opportunities for innovation and problem-solving, especially in industries like healthcare, e-commerce, finance, and customer service.

CHAPTER 18

SENTIMENT ANALYSIS WITH PYTHON

Introduction to Sentiment Analysis

Sentiment Analysis is a subfield of Natural Language Processing (NLP) that focuses on determining the sentiment or opinion expressed in a piece of text. The goal is to classify text into categories like **positive, negative,** or **neutral** based on the emotions or opinions conveyed. Sentiment analysis is widely used in various industries to analyze customer feedback, reviews, social media posts, and more.

Sentiment analysis can be broadly categorized into:

- **Binary Sentiment Analysis**: Classifies text as either positive or negative.
- **Multiclass Sentiment Analysis**: Classifies text into multiple sentiment categories, such as positive, negative, and neutral.
- **Fine-Grained Sentiment Analysis**: Involves more granular categories such as happy, angry, sad, or excited.

Applications of sentiment analysis include:

- **Customer Reviews**: Analyzing product reviews to determine whether customers have a positive or negative opinion.

- **Social Media Monitoring**: Monitoring social media platforms like Twitter or Facebook for sentiment toward a brand or product.

- **Market Research**: Understanding public sentiment toward companies or products to guide decision-making.

Building a Sentiment Analysis Model using Python

In this section, we will build a simple sentiment analysis model using Python. We will use **Scikit-learn** for machine learning, **NLTK** for text preprocessing, and **Pandas** for handling the dataset.

1. **Import Libraries**: We will start by importing the necessary libraries.

```python
import pandas as pd
import numpy as np
from    sklearn.model_selection    import
train_test_split
from        sklearn.feature_extraction.text
import CountVectorizer
```

```
from         sklearn.naive_bayes         import
MultinomialNB
from         sklearn.metrics         import
accuracy_score,     classification_report,
confusion_matrix
import nltk
```

2. **Loading and Preparing the Dataset**: For this example, we will use a sample dataset of text and sentiment labels. We will use a dataset containing movie reviews with sentiments labeled as "positive" or "negative".

```python
# Sample dataset
data = {
    'text': ['I love this movie', 'This
movie is terrible', 'Amazing film', 'I hate
this film', 'It was a great experience'],
    'sentiment': ['positive', 'negative',
'positive', 'negative', 'positive']
}

df = pd.DataFrame(data)

# Display the dataset
print(df)
```

3. **Preprocessing the Text**: We need to preprocess the text data by tokenizing the words, removing stopwords, and converting text into numerical format (feature vectors). We will use **CountVectorizer** to convert the text into a bag-of-words model.

```python
# Split the data into features (X) and
labels (y)
X = df['text']
y = df['sentiment']

# Convert text to a bag of words
(vectorization)
vectorizer                            =
CountVectorizer(stop_words='english')
X_vectorized = vectorizer.fit_transform(X)

# Split the data into training and testing
sets
X_train,   X_test,   y_train,   y_test   =
train_test_split(X_vectorized,          y,
test_size=0.3, random_state=42)

print(X_train.shape)   # Show the shape of
the feature vector after vectorization
```

4. **Building the Model**: We will use the **Multinomial Naive Bayes** algorithm, which is commonly used for text classification tasks such as sentiment analysis.

```python
python
```

```python
# Initialize the model
model = MultinomialNB()

# Train the model on the training data
model.fit(X_train, y_train)

# Predict on the test data
y_pred = model.predict(X_test)
```

5. **Evaluating the Model**: After making predictions, we can evaluate the model's performance using metrics like **accuracy**, **confusion matrix**, and **classification report**.

```python
python
```

```python
# Accuracy of the model
accuracy = accuracy_score(y_test, y_pred)
print(f'Accuracy: {accuracy * 100:.2f}%')

# Confusion Matrix
cm = confusion_matrix(y_test, y_pred)
print('Confusion Matrix:')
print(cm)
```

```
# Classification Report
report   =   classification_report(y_test,
y_pred)
print('Classification Report:')
print(report)
```

o **Accuracy**: Measures the percentage of correct predictions.

o **Confusion Matrix**: Shows the number of true positives, true negatives, false positives, and false negatives.

o **Classification Report**: Includes precision, recall, and F1-score for each class.

Evaluating Sentiment Analysis Models

When evaluating a sentiment analysis model, we focus on several key metrics that help us understand how well the model is performing:

1. **Accuracy**:

o **Definition**: Accuracy is the proportion of correct predictions (both positive and negative) to the total number of predictions.

o **Formula**:

Accuracy=Number of Correct PredictionsTotal Number of Predictions\text{Accuracy} = \frac{\text{Number of Correct Predictions}}{\text{Total Number of Predictions}}Accuracy=Total Number of Predictions Number of Correct Predictions

- o **Limitations**: Accuracy might not be enough, especially for imbalanced datasets where one class (e.g., "positive" sentiment) is more frequent than the other (e.g., "negative" sentiment).

2. **Precision**:

- o **Definition**: Precision measures how many of the predicted positive instances are actually positive.

Precision=TPTP+FP\text{Precision} = \frac{TP}{TP + FP}Precision=TP+FPTP

where:

- o **TP**: True Positives
- o **FP**: False Positives
- o **When to Use**: Precision is important when the cost of false positives is high (e.g., predicting a positive sentiment when it is actually negative).

3. **Recall (Sensitivity)**:

- o **Definition**: Recall measures how many of the actual positive instances were correctly predicted by the model.

$$\text{Recall} = \frac{TP}{TP + FN}$$

where:

- o **FN**: False Negatives
- o **When to Use**: Recall is important when the cost of false negatives is high (e.g., missing a positive sentiment).

4. **F1-Score**:
   - o **Definition**: The F1-score is the harmonic mean of precision and recall, providing a balance between the two.

$$\text{F1-score} = 2 \cdot \frac{\text{Precision} \cdot \text{Recall}}{\text{Precision} + \text{Recall}}$$

   - o **When to Use**: F1-score is particularly useful when you need to balance precision and recall, especially in imbalanced datasets.

5. **Confusion Matrix**:

- o The confusion matrix provides a detailed breakdown of the model's performance, showing:
  - **True Positives (TP)**: The number of positive instances correctly predicted as positive.
  - **False Positives (FP)**: The number of negative instances incorrectly predicted as positive.
  - **True Negatives (TN)**: The number of negative instances correctly predicted as negative.
  - **False Negatives (FN)**: The number of positive instances incorrectly predicted as negative.
- o **Example Confusion Matrix**:

```lua
[[15,  2],
 [ 3, 10]]
```

6. **ROC Curve and AUC**:
   - o **ROC Curve**: The ROC (Receiver Operating Characteristic) curve plots the **True Positive Rate (Recall)** against the **False Positive Rate**. The curve shows the performance of the model at various classification thresholds.

- AUC (Area Under the Curve): AUC is the area under the ROC curve. A higher AUC (close to 1) indicates a better performing model.
- Example of Plotting ROC Curve:

```python

from       sklearn.metrics       import
roc_curve, auc
import matplotlib.pyplot as plt

fpr,      tpr,      thresholds      =
roc_curve(y_test,
model.predict_proba(X_test)[:,1],
pos_label="positive")
roc_auc = auc(fpr, tpr)

plt.figure()
plt.plot(fpr,                    tpr,
color='darkorange', lw=2, label='ROC
curve (area = %0.2f)' % roc_auc)
plt.plot([0,     1],     [0,     1],
color='navy', lw=2, linestyle='--')
plt.xlim([0.0, 1.0])
plt.ylim([0.0, 1.05])
plt.xlabel('False Positive Rate')
plt.ylabel('True Positive Rate')
plt.title('Receiver         Operating
Characteristic (ROC) Curve')
```

179

```
plt.legend(loc="lower right")
plt.show()
```

Conclusion

In this chapter, we explored **Sentiment Analysis**, a key application of **Natural Language Processing (NLP)**, used to determine the sentiment expressed in text data. We walked through the steps of building a sentiment analysis model using Python, starting from text preprocessing (tokenization and vectorization) to training a **Multinomial Naive Bayes** classifier. We also discussed how to evaluate sentiment analysis models using metrics like **accuracy**, **precision**, **recall**, **F1-score**, and the **confusion matrix**.

Sentiment analysis is widely used in various industries, such as customer feedback analysis, social media monitoring, and market research. By applying these techniques, you can gain valuable insights from text data and build intelligent systems that understand and respond to human emotions and opinions.

CHAPTER 19

INTRODUCTION TO REINFORCEMENT LEARNING

What is Reinforcement Learning?

Reinforcement Learning (RL) is a type of machine learning where an **agent** learns to make decisions by interacting with an **environment**. The agent aims to maximize its cumulative **reward** over time by choosing actions that lead to positive outcomes. Unlike supervised learning, where the model learns from labeled data, in reinforcement learning, the agent learns through trial and error, receiving feedback in the form of rewards or penalties based on the actions it takes.

RL is based on the idea of **sequential decision-making**, where the agent's actions not only affect the immediate outcome but also influence future states and rewards. The agent explores the environment, makes decisions, and learns from those decisions to improve its future actions.

Key characteristics of reinforcement learning:

- **Learning from Interaction**: The agent learns by interacting with the environment and receiving feedback.

- **Exploration vs. Exploitation**: The agent faces a trade-off between exploring new actions (which may lead to better rewards) and exploiting known actions that have already yielded high rewards.

- **Delayed Rewards**: In RL, the reward for a given action may not be immediate, and the agent must often make decisions based on the long-term consequences of its actions.

The goal of reinforcement learning is to find an optimal policy, which is a strategy for selecting actions that maximizes the expected cumulative reward over time.

Key Concepts: Agents, Environments, Rewards

There are several key components in a reinforcement learning system:

1. **Agent**:
   - The **agent** is the learner or decision-maker. It interacts with the environment by taking actions and receiving feedback in the form of rewards.
   - The agent's objective is to learn the best strategy (policy) for selecting actions that maximize long-term rewards.
   - Example: A robot navigating a maze, a self-driving car, or a computer playing a game.

2. **Environment**:

   o The **environment** is everything the agent interacts with. It represents the external world the agent operates in.

   o The environment responds to the agent's actions and provides feedback (in the form of a new state and a reward) after each action.

   o Example: In a maze game, the environment includes the maze itself, the walls, the goal, and other obstacles.

3. **State**:

   o A **state** represents the current situation or configuration of the environment. The state provides the agent with information about the environment at a specific time.

   o Example: In a game, the state could include the position of the player, the score, or the game level.

4. **Action**:

   o An **action** is any move or decision the agent makes. The agent chooses actions based on the current state and aims to move toward an optimal outcome.

   o Example: In a board game, the action could be choosing a move (e.g., move a piece on the board).

5. **Reward**:

   o A **reward** is a numerical value the agent receives after taking an action in a particular state. The reward indicates how good or bad the action was in achieving the agent's goal.

   o Positive rewards encourage the agent to repeat the action, while negative rewards (or penalties) discourage it.

   o Example: In a video game, the agent may receive a positive reward for defeating an opponent and a negative reward for losing a life.

6. **Policy**:

   o A **policy** is a strategy that defines the agent's way of choosing actions given a state. It can be a simple rule or a more complex function learned through interaction with the environment.

   o In reinforcement learning, the goal is to learn the **optimal policy**, which maximizes the cumulative reward over time.

7. **Value Function**:

   o The **value function** estimates the expected long-term reward an agent can achieve from a given state, following a particular policy. It helps the agent evaluate how favorable a particular state is.

- The agent's objective is to maximize the total reward over time, which is influenced by the value of the states it visits.

8. **Q-Function (Action-Value Function)**:
   - The **Q-function** estimates the expected reward for taking a particular action in a particular state, and following the optimal policy thereafter. It is used in methods like **Q-Learning**.
   - The Q-value of a state-action pair tells the agent how much reward it can expect if it takes a certain action in a given state.

Real-World Applications of Reinforcement Learning

Reinforcement learning has many practical applications across various domains, from gaming and robotics to healthcare and finance. Here are some real-world examples:

1. **Gaming and Simulation**:
   - One of the most well-known applications of RL is in game-playing agents. Reinforcement learning algorithms like **Deep Q-Networks (DQN)** and **AlphaZero** have achieved superhuman performance in games like **Chess**, **Go**, and **Atari** games.
   - **AlphaGo**, developed by DeepMind, used RL techniques to defeat human world champions in

the game of Go, which was previously considered impossible for machines.

2. **Robotics**:

   o   RL is used in robotics to enable robots to learn tasks by interacting with their environment. Robots can learn to perform complex tasks like picking and placing objects, navigating through environments, or assembling products through trial and error.

   o   **Robotic arms** in manufacturing or warehouses use RL to optimize the movement and placement of objects.

3. **Self-Driving Cars**:

   o   In autonomous driving, RL is used to teach self-driving cars how to navigate through traffic, obey traffic laws, and respond to unexpected events (e.g., obstacles or roadblocks).

   o   By interacting with a simulated environment, the car learns the best actions to take in various traffic conditions, improving safety and efficiency.

4. **Healthcare**:

   o   RL has been applied in healthcare for personalized treatment planning, robotic surgery, and drug discovery. For example, RL can help optimize treatment regimens for patients with chronic diseases, ensuring that interventions are tailored to each individual's condition.

o **Drug Discovery**: Reinforcement learning can be used to optimize molecular structures for drug discovery, helping to find compounds that interact with biological targets in the most effective way.

5. **Finance and Trading**:

o In the finance industry, RL is used for portfolio management, algorithmic trading, and financial decision-making. Agents can be trained to learn strategies for buying and selling assets to maximize returns while minimizing risk.

o By simulating market conditions and observing past performance, an RL model can learn to make optimal trading decisions over time.

6. **Recommendation Systems**:

o Many recommendation systems (e.g., for movies, products, or content) use RL to personalize suggestions based on user preferences and feedback. The system continuously improves its recommendations based on user interactions, maximizing engagement and satisfaction.

7. **Industrial Automation and Supply Chain Optimization**:

o RL can be used to optimize supply chains, production lines, and logistics. Agents can learn the best strategies for scheduling tasks, managing inventories, and optimizing resource usage in manufacturing and distribution systems.

o **Smart grid management**: RL can help optimize the operation of electrical grids by learning the best actions to take in response to varying demand and supply.

8. **Advertising and Marketing**:

o RL can be used in advertising platforms to optimize bidding strategies for ad placements, maximizing return on investment (ROI). The agent learns to make decisions on how much to bid on ads based on user interaction and feedback.

Conclusion

In this chapter, we introduced **Reinforcement Learning (RL)**, a key area of machine learning that focuses on teaching agents to make decisions through interaction with an environment. We discussed the key components of an RL system, such as agents, environments, actions, rewards, and policies. We also explored real-world applications of RL in domains like gaming, robotics, self-driving cars, healthcare, finance, and more.

Reinforcement learning is a powerful tool for solving sequential decision-making problems, where the objective is to maximize long-term rewards through trial and error. As RL continues to advance, it is expected to play an increasingly important role in developing intelligent systems that can autonomously adapt to complex environments and tasks.

CHAPTER 20

BUILDING A SIMPLE REINFORCEMENT LEARNING MODEL

Introduction to Q-Learning

Q-Learning is a model-free **Reinforcement Learning (RL)** algorithm used to find the optimal policy for an agent interacting with an environment. Unlike other methods, Q-learning does not require knowledge of the environment's dynamics, making it highly flexible and useful for solving a variety of RL problems.

In Q-learning, the agent learns to choose actions in such a way that it maximizes the **total cumulative reward** over time. It does this by updating a **Q-table**, which stores the **Q-values** (action-value pairs). These Q-values represent the expected future rewards for taking a certain action in a given state and following the optimal policy thereafter.

The Q-value of a state-action pair $Q(s,a)Q(s, a)Q(s,a)$ is updated using the following **Bellman Equation**:

$Q(s_t,a_t) \leftarrow Q(s_t,a_t)+\alpha[r_{t+1}+\gamma \max_{a'} Q(s_{t+1},a')-Q(s_t,a_t)]Q(s\_t,$
$a\_t)$ \leftarrow Q(s_t, a_t) + \alpha \left[r_{t+1} + \gamma

\max_{a'} Q(s_{t+1}, a') - Q(s_t, a_t) \right]Q(st,at)←Q(st,at)+α[rt+1+γa'maxQ(st+1,a')−Q(st,at)]

Where:

- Q(st,at)Q(s_t, a_t)Q(st,at) is the current Q-value for state sts_tst and action ata_tat,
- α\alphaα is the **learning rate**, which controls how much new information overrides the old information,
- rt+1r_{t+1}rt+1 is the immediate reward received after taking action ata_tat,
- γ\gammaγ is the **discount factor**, which determines the importance of future rewards,
- max⁡a'Q(st+1,a')\max_{a'} Q(s_{t+1}, a')maxa'Q(st+1 ,a') is the maximum Q-value for the next state st+1s_{t+1}st+1, over all possible actions a'a'a'.

Through multiple iterations of exploring the environment and updating the Q-values, the agent learns the optimal policy (the sequence of actions that leads to the highest cumulative reward).

Building a Basic Reinforcement Learning Model

Now that we understand the basics of Q-learning, let's build a simple Q-learning model for a problem where the agent has to navigate a grid environment. In this example, the agent will move through the grid, trying to reach a goal while avoiding obstacles and collecting rewards.

1. **Import Necessary Libraries**: We will use **NumPy** for array manipulation and **random** for exploring the environment.

   python

   ```
   import numpy as np
   import random
   ```

2. **Setting Up the Environment**: Let's define a simple grid environment where the agent starts at the top-left corner, the goal is at the bottom-right corner, and the agent can move up, down, left, or right. The agent receives a positive reward for reaching the goal and a negative reward for hitting obstacles.

   python

   ```
   # Define the grid dimensions and rewards
   grid_size = 5  # 5x5 grid
   goal_state = (4, 4)  # Goal state at the
   bottom-right corner
   obstacle_states = [(2, 2), (1, 3)]  #
   Example obstacle locations

   # Initialize the Q-table (grid_size *
   grid_size states, 4 possible actions)
   Q = np.zeros((grid_size, grid_size, 4))  #
   4 actions: up, down, left, right
   ```

```python
# Define action space (0: up, 1: down, 2:
left, 3: right)
actions = [(0, -1), (0, 1), (-1, 0), (1,
0)]   # Move directions

# Define rewards for the environment
def get_reward(state):
    if state == goal_state:
        return 100   # Reward for reaching
the goal
    if state in obstacle_states:
        return -10   # Penalty for hitting
an obstacle
    return -1  # Penalty for each move
```

3. **Q-Learning Algorithm**: Now, let's implement the Q-learning algorithm to train the agent to find the optimal path to the goal.

python

```python
# Hyperparameters
learning_rate = 0.1 # Alpha: learning rate
discount_factor = 0.9  # Gamma: discount
factor
epsilon  =  0.1     #  Epsilon-greedy:
exploration rate
```

```python
episodes = 1000   # Number of training
episodes

# Training the agent
for episode in range(episodes):
    # Reset the environment: agent starts
at the top-left corner
    state = (0, 0)

    while state != goal_state:
        # Choose action: epsilon-greedy
strategy
        if random.uniform(0, 1) < epsilon:
            # Explore: select random
action
            action                     =
random.choice(range(4))
        else:
            # Exploit: select action with
max Q-value for current state
            action = np.argmax(Q[state[0],
state[1]])

        # Take action and observe the next
state
        next_state    =    (state[0]    +
actions[action][0],      state[1]      +
actions[action][1])
```

```
        # Ensure the next state is within
grid bounds
        if   next_state[0]   <   0   or
next_state[0]      >=      grid_size      or
next_state[1]  <  0  or  next_state[1]  >=
grid_size:
            next_state = state  # Stay in
the current state if out of bounds

        # Get the reward for the next state
        reward = get_reward(next_state)

        # Update  the  Q-value  using  the
Bellman Equation
        Q[state[0],  state[1],  action]  +=
learning_rate * (reward + discount_factor
*  np.max(Q[next_state[0],  next_state[1]])
- Q[state[0], state[1], action])

        # Move to the next state
        state = next_state
```

4. **Evaluating the Model's Performance**: After training the agent, we can evaluate its performance by checking the path it takes to reach the goal. We will use the learned Q-values to choose the optimal action at each step.

```python
python
```

```python
# Test the learned policy (finding the
optimal path)
state = (0, 0)
path = [state]

while state != goal_state:
    # Choose the action with the highest Q-
value for the current state
    action = np.argmax(Q[state[0],
state[1]])

    # Move to the next state based on the
selected action
    state = (state[0] +
actions[action][0], state[1] +
actions[action][1])

    # Ensure the state is within bounds
    if state[0] < 0 or state[0] >=
grid_size or state[1] < 0 or state[1] >=
grid_size:
        break

    path.append(state)

print("Optimal path:", path)
```

The model will output the optimal path the agent should take to reach the goal, based on the learned Q-values.

Conclusion

In this chapter, we introduced **Q-Learning**, a foundational algorithm in **Reinforcement Learning (RL)**. Q-learning enables an agent to learn an optimal policy for sequential decision-making by interacting with its environment and updating the **Q-values** based on the rewards it receives.

We walked through the process of building a basic reinforcement learning model where an agent learns to navigate a grid and reach a goal while avoiding obstacles. We implemented the Q-learning algorithm, set up the environment, and trained the agent through trial and error. Finally, we evaluated the model by testing the learned policy and finding the optimal path.

Reinforcement learning, and specifically Q-learning, is widely used in areas such as robotics, game playing, and autonomous decision-making. With further advancements, Q-learning can be scaled to handle more complex environments, such as multi-agent systems and high-dimensional state spaces.

CHAPTER 21

MODEL TUNING AND
OPTIMIZATION

Introduction to Hyperparameter Tuning

Hyperparameter tuning is a crucial step in the machine learning pipeline. It refers to the process of selecting the best set of hyperparameters for a machine learning model. Hyperparameters are the parameters that are set before training the model and are not learned from the data during training. They directly influence the model's learning process and performance.

For example:

- In **decision trees**, hyperparameters include the maximum depth of the tree, the minimum number of samples required to split a node, and the criterion for splitting nodes.
- In **neural networks**, hyperparameters include the learning rate, the number of hidden layers, and the number of neurons in each layer.
- In **support vector machines (SVM)**, hyperparameters include the penalty parameter (C) and the kernel type (linear, RBF, etc.).

Choosing the right hyperparameters can significantly improve the model's performance, while poor choices may lead to overfitting or underfitting.

Types of Hyperparameters:

- **Model hyperparameters**: These define the structure of the model (e.g., the depth of a decision tree, the number of hidden layers in a neural network).
- **Training hyperparameters**: These control the training process (e.g., the learning rate, batch size, number of epochs).
- **Optimization hyperparameters**: These affect the optimization algorithm (e.g., momentum in gradient descent, learning rate decay).

Goal of Hyperparameter Tuning: The goal is to find the combination of hyperparameters that leads to the best model performance on unseen data, typically by maximizing accuracy or minimizing error. This can be done through different methods like **grid search**, **randomized search**, and using **cross-validation**.

Grid Search and Randomized Search

1. **Grid Search**:
   o **Definition**: Grid search is a brute-force approach to hyperparameter tuning, where you specify a set of hyperparameter values, and the algorithm

exhaustively tests all possible combinations of these hyperparameters.

- o **How it Works**:
  - You define a grid of hyperparameter values for each hyperparameter you want to tune.
  - The model is trained and evaluated for every possible combination of hyperparameters in the grid.
  - The combination of hyperparameters that yields the best performance (based on cross-validation) is selected.
- o **Pros**:
  - Simple to understand and implement.
  - Guaranteed to find the best combination of hyperparameters (within the grid).
- o **Cons**:
  - Can be computationally expensive, especially for models with many hyperparameters or large datasets.
  - It may search through many unnecessary hyperparameter combinations, leading to inefficiency.

Example of Grid Search in Python:

```python
python
```

```python
from sklearn.model_selection import GridSearchCV
from sklearn.ensemble import RandomForestClassifier

# Define the model
model = RandomForestClassifier()

# Define the hyperparameters grid
param_grid = {
    'n_estimators': [50, 100, 200],
    'max_depth': [10, 20, None],
    'min_samples_split': [2, 5, 10]
}

# Apply Grid Search with 5-fold cross-validation
grid_search = GridSearchCV(estimator=model, param_grid=param_grid, cv=5, n_jobs=-1, verbose=2)

# Fit the model
grid_search.fit(X_train, y_train)

# Best parameters and score
print("Best Hyperparameters:", grid_search.best_params_)
```

```
print("Best     Cross-validation     Score:",
grid_search.best_score_)
```

2. **Randomized Search**:
   - **Definition**: Randomized search is an alternative to grid search that randomly samples hyperparameters from a specified distribution or set of values. Instead of testing all combinations, it randomly selects combinations, often over a large number of trials, which can make the process more efficient.
   - **How it Works**:
     - Instead of trying all combinations like grid search, randomized search tests random combinations of hyperparameters for a given number of iterations.
     - This approach is much faster, especially when dealing with large parameter grids.
   - **Pros**:
     - More efficient than grid search, as it doesn't test every combination.
     - Can lead to good results even when not all hyperparameters are tested.
   - **Cons**:
     - There is no guarantee that the best combination of hyperparameters will be

found, especially if the number of iterations is small.

Example of Randomized Search in Python:

python

```
from    sklearn.model_selection    import
RandomizedSearchCV
from         sklearn.ensemble       import
RandomForestClassifier
from scipy.stats import randint

# Define the model
model = RandomForestClassifier()

# Define the hyperparameters distribution
param_dist = {
    'n_estimators': randint(50, 200),
    'max_depth': [10, 20, None],
    'min_samples_split': randint(2, 10)
}

# Apply Randomized Search with 5-fold
cross-validation
random_search                        =
RandomizedSearchCV(estimator=model,
param_distributions=param_dist,
```

203

```
n_iter=100,          cv=5,           n_jobs=-1,
random_state=42, verbose=2)


# Fit the model
random_search.fit(X_train, y_train)


# Best parameters and score
print("Best            Hyperparameters:",
random_search.best_params_)
print("Best   Cross-validation   Score:",
random_search.best_score_)
```

In this example, `randint` from `scipy.stats` is used to randomly sample integer values for hyperparameters.

Using Cross-Validation for Model Tuning

Cross-validation is a technique used to evaluate a model's performance by splitting the dataset into multiple subsets (folds) and training/testing the model on different splits. Cross-validation is particularly useful for hyperparameter tuning as it helps assess how well the model generalizes to unseen data.

K-Fold Cross-Validation:

- **Definition**: In k-fold cross-validation, the dataset is split into **K** equal-sized folds. The model is trained on $K-1$K-1$K-1$ folds and evaluated on the remaining fold. This process is repeated KKK times, with each fold serving as the test set once.

- **Purpose**: Cross-validation helps to ensure that the model's performance is not overly optimistic due to overfitting on a particular split of the data.

Using Cross-Validation for Hyperparameter Tuning: When tuning a model using grid search or randomized search, **cross-validation** is used to estimate the performance of different hyperparameter combinations. It allows for better generalization and helps avoid overfitting to a particular training set.

Here's how you can combine **cross-validation** with **grid search** or **randomized search** to tune the model's hyperparameters:

1. **Grid Search with Cross-Validation**: In the earlier grid search example, the `cv=5` parameter specifies 5-fold cross-validation. Grid search evaluates each hyperparameter combination using cross-validation to provide a more robust performance estimate.

2. **Randomized Search with Cross-Validation**: Similarly, the `RandomizedSearchCV` also supports cross-validation with the `cv` parameter, ensuring that each random combination of hyperparameters is evaluated across multiple folds.

Conclusion

In this chapter, we explored the importance of **model tuning** and **optimization** in machine learning. Hyperparameter tuning is a crucial step to improve the performance of machine learning models. We introduced two powerful techniques for hyperparameter tuning: **Grid Search** and **Randomized Search**, both of which help us find the best hyperparameter values by systematically exploring different options.

Additionally, we discussed the role of **cross-validation** in model evaluation and tuning. By incorporating cross-validation into the tuning process, we ensure that our models are not overfitting to a specific training set and are generalizing well to unseen data.

Mastering these techniques can significantly improve the performance of machine learning models and allow for better generalization, making them more reliable for real-world applications.

CHAPTER 22

INTRODUCTION TO MODEL DEPLOYMENT

Why Deploy Machine Learning Models?

Model deployment is the process of integrating a machine learning model into a production environment where it can be accessed and used by end-users or other systems. The primary goal of deploying machine learning models is to make the predictive power of the model available in real-world applications. By deploying models, organizations can leverage machine learning to automate decision-making, provide real-time insights, improve processes, and enhance user experiences.

Key Reasons for Deploying Machine Learning Models:

1. **Real-Time Predictions**: Once a model is deployed, it can generate predictions based on live data in real-time, enabling applications to take immediate actions (e.g., fraud detection, recommendation systems).

2. **Automation**: Model deployment can automate decision-making processes, such as classifying images, detecting anomalies, or recommending products, reducing manual effort and improving efficiency.

3. **Scalability**: A deployed model can be used to serve predictions to thousands or millions of users without human intervention, making it scalable and suitable for large applications.

4. **Integration with Business Applications**: Deployed models can be integrated with other business systems (e.g., CRM systems, financial platforms, or healthcare applications) to make data-driven decisions and insights available directly in the business workflows.

5. **Continuous Improvement**: Once deployed, models can be monitored and updated based on real-time data to continuously improve performance.

By deploying a machine learning model, organizations can provide valuable services, improve decision-making, and drive innovation.

Types of Model Deployment (Batch vs Real-Time)

There are two common approaches for deploying machine learning models: **batch deployment** and **real-time deployment**. The choice between the two depends on the nature of the application and the business needs.

1. **Batch Deployment**:
   - **Definition**: In **batch deployment**, the model is deployed to process large batches of data at

periodic intervals. The model makes predictions or decisions on the entire dataset at once, and the results are processed in bulk.

- **Use Cases**: Batch processing is suitable for scenarios where real-time predictions are not necessary, and data can be processed in bulk at scheduled times (e.g., daily or weekly). Common use cases include:
  - Processing data for trend analysis.
  - Updating customer segmentation models.
  - Running reports or aggregating data for analytics purposes.
- **Advantages**:
  - Easier to implement and manage.
  - Less computational overhead per prediction, as the model processes data in bulk.
  - Suitable for use cases that do not require immediate decision-making.
- **Disadvantages**:
  - Cannot provide real-time insights or decisions.
  - Time lag between when data is collected and when predictions are made.

Example: A company might run a batch job every night to update product recommendations based on user activity from the past 24 hours.

2. **Real-Time Deployment**:
   o **Definition**: In **real-time deployment**, the model is used to generate predictions instantly or with minimal delay as new data arrives. This deployment approach is used when immediate decisions are required based on fresh, incoming data.
   o **Use Cases**: Real-time deployment is suitable for applications that need to make decisions immediately, such as:
     ▪ Fraud detection in financial transactions.
     ▪ Personalized content recommendation in real-time.
     ▪ Autonomous vehicle decision-making.
     ▪ Predicting customer churn as soon as new customer interactions are recorded.
   o **Advantages**:
     ▪ Provides immediate insights and actions.
     ▪ Suitable for applications that require dynamic responses to incoming data.
   o **Disadvantages**:
     ▪ Requires more computational resources to serve predictions in real-time.

- More complex to implement and maintain, especially for high-throughput systems.
- Possible latency issues if the system is not well-optimized.

Example: A real-time recommendation system that suggests products to users as they browse an e-commerce website.

Deploying Models Using Flask or FastAPI

Once you've trained and fine-tuned your machine learning model, the next step is to deploy it so that it can be accessed by other applications. Two popular frameworks for deploying machine learning models in Python are **Flask** and **FastAPI**. Both are lightweight web frameworks that allow you to build API endpoints to serve predictions from your model.

1. **Flask**:
   - **Flask** is a micro web framework for Python that allows you to build simple web applications and APIs. It is widely used for deploying machine learning models in production due to its simplicity and ease of use.
   - **Steps to Deploy a Model with Flask**:
     1. **Install Flask**: Install Flask using pip.

```bash
bash

pip install Flask
```

2. **Create the Flask Application**: Set up a basic Flask app that serves a machine learning model.

```python
python

from flask import Flask,
request, jsonify
import joblib  # For loading
the model

app = Flask(__name__)

# Load the trained model
(ensure the model is saved as
a .pkl or .joblib file)
model                     =
joblib.load('model.pkl')

# Define the API endpoint
@app.route('/predict',
methods=['POST'])
def predict():
    # Get the data from the
POST request
```

212

```
    data                    =
request.get_json(force=True)
    # Extract the features
    features                =
data['features']
    # Make the prediction
    prediction              =
model.predict([features])
    # Return the prediction as
JSON
    return
jsonify(prediction=prediction
[0])

if __name__ == '__main__':
    app.run(debug=True)
```

3. **Testing the API**: After running the Flask app, you can send a **POST request** with the input data (features) to get predictions. You can use **Postman** or **cURL** for testing.

```bash
bash
```

```bash
curl -X POST -H "Content-Type:
application/json" \
-d '{"features": [feature1,
feature2, feature3]}' \
```

213

```
http://localhost:5000/predict
```

2. **Advantages of Flask**:
   o   Simple and lightweight.
   o   Great for small applications or quick prototypes.
   o   Highly flexible and easy to extend.

3. **FastAPI**:

   o   **FastAPI** is another web framework for Python that is designed to be faster and more efficient than Flask, especially for APIs that require high performance. FastAPI is built on top of **Starlette** for the web parts and **Pydantic** for data validation.

   o   **Steps to Deploy a Model with FastAPI**:

   1. **Install FastAPI** and **Uvicorn** (ASGI server for FastAPI).

   bash

   ```bash
   pip install fastapi uvicorn
   ```

   2. **Create the FastAPI Application**:

   python

   ```python
   from fastapi import FastAPI
   from pydantic import BaseModel
   import joblib
   ```

```python
app = FastAPI()

# Load the trained model
model                   =
joblib.load('model.pkl')

# Define the input data model
class Item(BaseModel):
    features: list

# Define the prediction
endpoint
@app.post("/predict")
def predict(item: Item):
    # Get the features from the
request
    features = item.features
    # Make the prediction
    prediction              =
model.predict([features])
    return       {"prediction":
prediction[0]}

if __name__ == "__main__":
    import uvicorn
    uvicorn.run(app,
host="0.0.0.0", port=8000)
```

3. **Run the FastAPI Application**:

215

```bash
bash

uvicorn app:app --reload
```

This will start a server on http://localhost:8000.

4. **Testing the API**: You can send a POST request with the input data to the /predict endpoint just like with Flask.

```bash
bash

curl -X POST -H "Content-Type: application/json" \
-d '{"features": [feature1, feature2, feature3]}' \
http://localhost:8000/predict
```

4. **Advantages of FastAPI**:
   o Faster than Flask, especially for high-load applications.
   o Automatic API documentation with **Swagger UI**.
   o Supports asynchronous programming (asynchronous endpoints for high concurrency).
   o Built-in data validation using **Pydantic**.

Conclusion

In this chapter, we discussed the importance of **model deployment** and the steps required to deploy machine learning models in a production environment. We explored the difference between **batch** and **real-time deployment**, highlighting when each approach is appropriate.

We also introduced two popular frameworks for deploying machine learning models: **Flask** and **FastAPI**. Both frameworks allow you to create API endpoints that serve model predictions, with FastAPI being more optimized for high performance and scalability.

Model deployment is an essential part of the machine learning lifecycle, as it enables the model to be used in real-world applications. Whether you are building a web application, a recommendation system, or an automated decision-making process, deploying your model allows you to provide value and integrate machine learning into operational workflows.

CHAPTER 23

WORKING WITH REAL-TIME DATA

Handling Streaming Data

In today's world, many applications require real-time processing of data. Streaming data refers to data that is continuously generated and must be processed in real-time or near-real-time. Examples of streaming data include social media feeds, IoT sensor data, financial market data, and web traffic logs. Handling streaming data effectively is crucial for real-time decision-making, predictive analytics, and automated systems.

Challenges of Streaming Data:

- **High Velocity**: Streaming data comes in at a high speed, often at thousands or millions of data points per second.
- **Infinite or Large Volumes**: Unlike static datasets, streaming data can be endless. Storing and processing such large volumes efficiently is critical.
- **Real-Time Processing**: Unlike batch processing, which can be done periodically, streaming data requires continuous processing with low latency.

- **Data Quality**: Streaming data might be noisy or incomplete, requiring real-time cleaning and validation.

Key Techniques for Handling Streaming Data:

1. **Windowing**:
   o Data is processed in **windows** of a fixed size or time duration (e.g., processing the last 5 minutes of data).
   o This allows for handling large data volumes without overwhelming the system.
   o Two common windowing techniques:
     - **Tumbling Windows**: Fixed-size non-overlapping windows.
     - **Sliding Windows**: Fixed-size windows that overlap with each other.

2. **Real-Time Data Aggregation**:
   o Aggregating data on the fly to derive insights, such as calculating rolling averages, counts, or sums over time.
   o This can help reduce the amount of data that needs to be stored while retaining important metrics.

3. **Data Filtering and Transformation**:
   o Filtering out unnecessary data points or transforming incoming data into a useful format

in real time is essential to reduce noise and improve model accuracy.

4. **Fault Tolerance**:

    o   Ensuring that data is not lost in case of system failures, which is critical for streaming systems. This can involve techniques like **checkpointing** and **data replication**.

Technologies for Handling Streaming Data:

- **Apache Kafka**: A distributed messaging system designed for high-throughput, fault-tolerant data streaming. Kafka is commonly used for collecting and managing large streams of data.

- **Apache Flink** and **Apache Spark Streaming**: Frameworks designed for processing large-scale streaming data in real-time.

- **Amazon Kinesis**: A cloud service provided by AWS for handling streaming data, often used with AWS Lambda for real-time processing.

- **Google Cloud Pub/Sub**: A messaging service for ingesting real-time data streams on Google Cloud.

Building Real-Time Data Processing Pipelines

A **real-time data processing pipeline** is a sequence of steps or stages that handle data from ingestion through to processing, storage, and eventual analysis. These pipelines are crucial for making sense of streaming data and enabling real-time analytics, decision-making, and predictions.

Components of a Real-Time Data Processing Pipeline:

1. **Data Ingestion**:
   o **Data sources** can include IoT devices, social media streams, user activity logs, sensor data, and more.
   o Data is typically ingested in **real-time** using message queues like Kafka, Pub/Sub, or streaming services like Kinesis.

2. **Data Processing**:
   o The next step involves processing the incoming data in real time. This may involve transformations, aggregation, filtering, enrichment, or applying machine learning models.
   o **Stream Processing Frameworks** like **Apache Flink**, **Apache Storm**, or **Apache Spark Streaming** are often used here to process data in real-time.

3. **Storage**:
   o Processed data might be stored temporarily in **data lakes** or **NoSQL databases** for further analysis or reporting.

- o **Time-series databases** (like **InfluxDB**) or distributed storage systems like **Hadoop** may be used for handling large volumes of time-ordered data.

4. **Real-Time Analytics**:
   - o The processed data can be analyzed in real time to generate insights, such as detecting anomalies, predicting trends, or providing recommendations.
   - o **Real-Time Dashboards** can be used to visualize this data and provide decision-makers with immediate feedback.

5. **Model Integration**:
   - o Real-time data can be passed to machine learning models for inference and decision-making. For example, a recommendation system might use real-time user behavior to suggest products or content.

6. **Output and Action**:
   - o After processing and analysis, the pipeline outputs actionable results. For instance, it could trigger an alert, update a dashboard, or execute a trade in a stock market system.

Example of a Simple Real-Time Pipeline:

1. **Data Ingestion**: A streaming service like Apache Kafka collects live traffic data from users.

222

2. **Data Processing**: Apache Flink processes the incoming data to identify users who are likely to churn based on their recent behavior.

3. **Model Deployment**: The processed data is sent to a pre-trained machine learning model that predicts whether a user is likely to churn.

4. **Action**: If the model predicts a user is likely to churn, the system sends a recommendation to the marketing team to target that user with a special offer.

Tools for Building Real-Time Pipelines:

- **Apache Kafka**: For reliable data ingestion and stream processing.

- **Apache Flink/Spark Streaming**: For real-time data processing and transformations.

- **Kubernetes**: For deploying scalable real-time services in cloud environments.

- **AWS Lambda/Google Cloud Functions**: For serverless real-time data processing.

- **Grafana/Power BI**: For building real-time dashboards and visualizations.

Integrating Machine Learning Models with Real-Time Data

Integrating machine learning models into a real-time data pipeline is one of the most powerful ways to make immediate, data-driven decisions. In this section, we will explore how machine learning models can be deployed and used within real-time systems.

Steps to Integrate Machine Learning Models with Real-Time Data:

1. **Train the Machine Learning Model**:
   o Train your machine learning model on historical data and fine-tune it for the problem at hand (e.g., classification, regression, anomaly detection).
   o For real-time applications, models should be lightweight and fast, so they can make predictions quickly.

2. **Model Deployment**:
   o Deploy the trained machine learning model as a service or API. Common tools for deploying models include:
      ▪ **Flask/FastAPI**: For serving models as RESTful APIs.
      ▪ **TensorFlow Serving**: A dedicated service for deploying TensorFlow models.
      ▪ **ONNX Runtime**: For serving models in multiple frameworks.
   o The model should be capable of handling incoming requests with low latency, providing real-time predictions.

224

3. **Real-Time Data Ingestion**:

   o Set up a streaming data source (e.g., Kafka, Kinesis) to feed real-time data into the model.

   o As new data arrives, it should be passed through the model for inference.

4. **Model Inference**:

   o Once the model is deployed, each new data point can be fed into the model for prediction. For instance, an IoT sensor's reading could be passed to a model predicting equipment failure or a user's behavior could be processed by a recommendation system.

   o The model provides an output (e.g., predicted class, value, or score).

5. **Action Based on Predictions**:

   o After obtaining predictions, the system should take appropriate action, such as:

   - Triggering an alert (e.g., in anomaly detection).

   - Making a recommendation (e.g., in content personalization).

   - Automatically taking actions (e.g., in financial trading systems).

6. **Model Monitoring and Updating**:

- o Models in production should be continuously monitored to ensure they are providing accurate predictions.

- o Over time, the model's performance may degrade due to changes in the data distribution (a phenomenon known as **concept drift**). Retraining the model on new data or using techniques like **online learning** can help maintain the model's accuracy.

Example: Real-Time Fraud Detection:

1. **Data Ingestion**: Financial transactions from users are streamed in real-time via Apache Kafka.
2. **Model Deployment**: A machine learning model for fraud detection is deployed using Flask. The model predicts whether a transaction is fraudulent or not.
3. **Prediction**: As a new transaction arrives, the data is processed and passed to the model for prediction.
4. **Action**: If the model predicts the transaction is fraudulent, the system immediately blocks the transaction and sends an alert to the user.

Tools for Integrating Machine Learning Models:

- • **TensorFlow Serving**: For serving TensorFlow models.
- • **Flask/FastAPI**: For serving models as APIs.

- **Kafka**: For managing streaming data ingestion.
- **Kubernetes**: For deploying scalable machine learning services.
- **MLflow**: For managing and deploying machine learning models in real-time pipelines.

Conclusion

In this chapter, we explored the challenges and techniques involved in working with **real-time data**. We discussed how to handle streaming data, build real-time data processing pipelines, and integrate machine learning models into these pipelines for immediate decision-making. Real-time data processing is crucial for applications that require fast, automated responses, such as fraud detection, recommendation systems, and dynamic pricing.

By building efficient data processing pipelines and integrating machine learning models, businesses can leverage real-time data to enhance user experiences, make data-driven decisions, and automate complex processes. As streaming data becomes increasingly prevalent, understanding how to process and act on this data in real-time will continue to be a key skill in modern data science and machine learning.

CHAPTER 24

MODEL EVALUATION AND IMPROVEMENT

Analyzing Model Errors

Once a machine learning model is trained and deployed, it's crucial to evaluate its performance and identify areas for improvement. **Analyzing model errors** is an essential part of the model evaluation process, as it helps to uncover weaknesses in the model, biases in the data, or incorrect assumptions made during training. By understanding where and why the model is making mistakes, you can take targeted actions to improve its performance.

There are several common types of errors that machine learning models can make:

1. **False Positives (Type I Error):**
   o This occurs when the model incorrectly classifies a negative instance as positive.
   o **Example**: In a fraud detection system, a false positive occurs when the model flags a legitimate transaction as fraudulent.
2. **False Negatives (Type II Error):**

- o This occurs when the model incorrectly classifies a positive instance as negative.
- o **Example**: In the same fraud detection system, a false negative occurs when the model fails to flag a fraudulent transaction.

3. **Bias**:

- o Bias refers to errors that are systematic and often occur when the model has certain assumptions or preferences that are incorrect.
- o **Example**: A model trained on biased data may predict certain outcomes more frequently for specific groups, leading to unfair predictions.

4. **Variance**:

- o Variance refers to errors that occur due to a model being too sensitive to the fluctuations or noise in the training data. High variance typically means the model overfits the training data and fails to generalize well to new, unseen data.

5. **Underfitting**:

- o Underfitting occurs when the model is too simple and fails to capture the underlying patterns in the data. It leads to poor performance on both training and testing datasets.
- o **Example**: A linear regression model that tries to predict a non-linear relationship may underfit the data.

229

Techniques for Analyzing Errors:

- **Confusion Matrix**: A confusion matrix is a tool that helps visualize the performance of classification models by showing the number of true positives, true negatives, false positives, and false negatives. It allows you to quickly see where the model is making errors.

```python
from       sklearn.metrics       import
confusion_matrix
cm = confusion_matrix(y_test, y_pred)
print(cm)
```

- **Cross-Validation**: Cross-validation provides a better estimate of model performance by splitting the data into multiple subsets and training the model on different portions. This helps to identify if the model is overfitting or underfitting.
- **Learning Curves**: Plotting learning curves (training and validation loss or accuracy over time) can help you diagnose issues with underfitting or overfitting.
- **Residual Analysis**: For regression tasks, analyzing residuals (differences between predicted and actual values) can help detect biases and issues in model assumptions.

Techniques for Improving Model Accuracy

After identifying the errors made by the model, the next step is to improve its accuracy. There are several techniques you can employ to boost model performance:

1. **Feature Engineering**:
   o **Adding more relevant features**: The quality and quantity of features can have a significant impact on model performance. By adding relevant features or creating new ones, you can provide the model with better information to make predictions.
   o **Feature scaling**: Some algorithms (e.g., SVM, k-NN, neural networks) require features to be on the same scale to perform optimally. Normalizing or standardizing features can help improve model performance.
   o **Feature selection**: Removing irrelevant or redundant features can help the model focus on the most important information, leading to better generalization.

2. **Model Complexity**:
   o **Increasing Model Complexity**: For underfitting models, increasing the complexity (e.g., adding more layers to a neural network or using a more complex algorithm like Random Forests) can

help the model better capture the underlying data patterns.

- o **Decreasing Model Complexity**: For overfitting models, reducing the complexity (e.g., decreasing the number of features or using simpler models) can help the model generalize better.

3. **Data Augmentation**:

- o In some cases, particularly with image or text data, augmenting the dataset (by generating new data from existing samples) can improve model performance by increasing the diversity of the training data.

- o **Example**: In image classification tasks, data augmentation techniques like rotation, flipping, and scaling can create additional training samples.

4. **Ensemble Methods**:

- o **Bagging**: Techniques like **Random Forests** use ensemble methods to combine multiple models and reduce variance by averaging the results.

- o **Boosting**: Methods like **AdaBoost** and **XGBoost** iteratively train models by focusing on the hardest-to-predict instances, which can help improve accuracy.

- o **Stacking**: Stacking involves training multiple models and combining their predictions with a meta-model. This approach often leads to better performance than any single model.

5. **Hyperparameter Tuning**:

   o Tuning hyperparameters (such as learning rate, number of trees, depth of decision trees, etc.) can help improve model accuracy. Techniques like **Grid Search** and **Randomized Search** can be used to find the best hyperparameters.

6. **Cross-Validation**:

   o Cross-validation helps ensure that the model is not overfitting or underfitting. By splitting the data into different subsets for training and testing, cross-validation gives a better estimate of model performance and can help identify potential issues.

Regularization Methods to Prevent Overfitting

Overfitting occurs when a model learns the details and noise in the training data to the extent that it negatively impacts the performance on new, unseen data. Regularization techniques are used to prevent overfitting by penalizing complex models and forcing them to generalize better.

1. **L1 Regularization (Lasso)**:

   o **Definition**: L1 regularization adds the absolute value of the coefficients (weights) to the loss function. This results in some coefficients being driven to zero, effectively performing **feature selection** by removing irrelevant features.

o **Formula**:

$$L1 = \lambda \sum_{i=1}^{n} |w_i|$$

o **Use Case**: L1 regularization is particularly useful when you have many features and you want to reduce the complexity by removing irrelevant ones.

2. **L2 Regularization (Ridge)**:

o **Definition**: L2 regularization adds the square of the coefficients to the loss function. It penalizes large coefficients but does not eliminate them completely. It helps prevent the model from fitting noise in the data.

o **Formula**:

$$L2 = \lambda \sum_{i=1}^{n} w_i^2$$

o **Use Case**: L2 regularization works well when you want to penalize large weights without completely eliminating them, making it effective for regression and classification models.

3. **Elastic Net**:

   o **Definition**: Elastic Net is a combination of both L1 and L2 regularization. It balances the sparsity of L1 with the stability of L2 regularization.

   o **Formula**:

   Elastic Net=λ(α∑i=1n|wi|+(1−α)∑i=1nwi2)\text {Elastic Net} = \lambda \left(\alpha \sum_{i=1}^{n} |w_i| + (1 - \alpha) \sum_{i=1}^{n} w_i^2 \right)Elastic Net=λ(αi=1∑n|wi|+(1−α)i=1∑n wi2)

   o **Use Case**: Elastic Net is useful when you have many correlated features and need the benefits of both L1 and L2 regularization.

4. **Dropout (for Neural Networks)**:

   o **Definition**: Dropout is a regularization technique used in deep learning, where random units (neurons) are "dropped" (set to zero) during training. This prevents the model from becoming too dependent on specific neurons and helps it generalize better.

   o **Use Case**: Dropout is particularly effective for deep neural networks where the risk of overfitting is high due to the complexity of the model.

5. **Early Stopping (for Neural Networks)**:

235

o **Definition**: Early stopping is a technique used in training neural networks where the training process is halted when the model's performance on the validation set stops improving. This prevents the model from overfitting by training for too many epochs.

o **Use Case**: Early stopping is often used in iterative models like deep learning, where continued training can lead to overfitting.

Conclusion

In this chapter, we discussed the key aspects of **model evaluation and improvement**. We explored how to analyze model errors, identify the types of mistakes a model makes, and use various techniques to improve its accuracy. Additionally, we covered **regularization methods** that help prevent overfitting, such as L1 and L2 regularization, Elastic Net, and Dropout.

Improving a machine learning model involves a continuous process of diagnosing issues, tuning hyperparameters, and using regularization to help the model generalize better to new, unseen data. By understanding these techniques and applying them appropriately, you can build more robust models that perform well in real-world applications.

CHAPTER 25

ETHICAL CONSIDERATIONS IN MACHINE LEARNING

Bias in Machine Learning Models

Bias in machine learning models refers to systematic errors introduced into the model that result from prejudiced assumptions or flawed data. This bias can have significant negative consequences, including unfair or discriminatory outcomes. Understanding and mitigating bias is crucial for developing ethical machine learning models, especially when models are used to make decisions affecting individuals or communities.

Types of Bias in Machine Learning:

1. **Data Bias**:
    - o **Definition**: Bias that arises from unrepresentative, incomplete, or skewed data. If the training data does not accurately represent the target population or the real-world scenario, the model is likely to produce biased results.
    - o **Example**: If a facial recognition model is trained primarily on images of light-skinned individuals,

it may perform poorly when applied to darker-skinned individuals.

2. **Algorithmic Bias**:

   o **Definition**: Bias that is introduced by the model's design or the learning process. Some algorithms may inherently favor certain outcomes or groups due to the mathematical assumptions or optimizations they rely on.

   o **Example**: A credit scoring model that uses variables like zip codes could introduce racial bias if certain zip codes are correlated with racial groups.

3. **Label Bias**:

   o **Definition**: Bias that arises when human annotators introduce subjective judgments when labeling data. In supervised learning, label bias can lead to incorrect predictions, especially when the labels themselves are biased.

   o **Example**: In sentiment analysis, human annotators may label a review as "negative" because they personally disagree with the sentiment expressed in the review.

4. **Sampling Bias**:

   o **Definition**: Bias that arises when the data sample does not represent the full population. If the sample over-represents one group while under-representing others, the model may not generalize well to the broader population.

- o **Example**: A health prediction model trained on data from a specific age group may fail to predict accurately for other age groups.

How Bias Affects Model Outcomes:

- **Discrimination**: Biased models may treat certain groups unfairly, leading to discriminatory outcomes.
- **Inequality**: Bias can exacerbate social inequalities by making decisions that disadvantage already marginalized groups.
- **Lack of Trust**: If stakeholders or the public perceive models as biased or unfair, they may lose trust in the technology and its use.

Fairness, Transparency, and Accountability in AI

Fairness:

- **Definition**: Fairness in AI refers to the principle that machine learning models should treat all individuals or groups equally and avoid favoring one group over another.
- **Challenges**:

o Defining fairness is complex because different stakeholders may have different views on what constitutes fairness.

o It is important to consider **distributive fairness** (e.g., equal access to benefits) and **procedural fairness** (e.g., fairness in decision-making processes).

Approaches to Fairness:

o **Equality of Opportunity**: Ensures that all groups have an equal chance of receiving positive outcomes.

o **Equalized Odds**: Ensures that the model's error rates (false positives and false negatives) are similar across different groups.

o **Demographic Parity**: Ensures that the model makes positive predictions at similar rates across different groups.

Transparency:

- **Definition**: Transparency refers to the ability to understand how a machine learning model works and how decisions are made. Transparency is essential for building trust and ensuring that AI systems can be audited and reviewed for fairness.

- **Challenges**:
  - Many machine learning models, especially deep learning models, are considered "black boxes," making it difficult to explain how they arrive at a particular decision.

Approaches to Transparency:

  - **Explainable AI (XAI)**: Techniques and methods that aim to make AI systems more interpretable. For example, methods like **LIME** (Local Interpretable Model-agnostic Explanations) and **SHAP** (Shapley Additive Explanations) can help explain the output of complex models.
  - **Model Documentation**: Providing clear documentation on how a model was built, the data it was trained on, and its limitations.

Accountability:

- **Definition**: Accountability refers to ensuring that there are clear mechanisms for holding individuals or organizations responsible for the decisions made by machine learning models. This is crucial when models are used in high-stakes applications like healthcare, finance, or criminal justice.
- **Challenges**:

- o It may be difficult to assign accountability when decisions are made by automated systems that are hard to explain or audit.

Approaches to Accountability:

- o **Model Audits**: Regularly auditing models to ensure they are functioning as expected and are not biased or discriminatory.
- o **Clear Ownership**: Identifying who is responsible for model development, deployment, and monitoring.

How to Build Ethical Machine Learning Models

Building ethical machine learning models involves proactively addressing issues related to fairness, transparency, and accountability during every stage of the model's lifecycle—from data collection to deployment. Here are some strategies to ensure that your machine learning models are ethical:

1. **Data Collection and Preprocessing**:
    - o **Diverse and Representative Data**: Ensure that the data used for training is representative of the population the model will serve. This helps minimize bias and ensures fairness.
    - o **Data Annotation**: When labeling data, ensure that the process is unbiased and that different

annotators have clear, objective guidelines to prevent label bias.

o **Bias Detection**: Use statistical methods to detect bias in your data before training the model. Tools like **Fairness Indicators** or **AI Fairness 360** can help assess and mitigate bias in datasets.

2. **Model Selection and Training**:

o **Fairness-Aware Algorithms**: Choose algorithms that promote fairness. Many machine learning libraries offer fairness metrics and adjustments. For example, **fairness constraints** can be incorporated into models to ensure that predictions are equitable across groups.

o **Regularization**: Use regularization techniques (like L1/L2 regularization) to prevent overfitting and ensure that models do not learn spurious correlations that could lead to biased decisions.

o **Cross-Validation**: Use cross-validation to assess how well your model generalizes and to detect potential overfitting, which could lead to discriminatory performance on certain groups.

3. **Model Evaluation and Testing**:

o **Performance Metrics for Fairness**: Evaluate your model using metrics that assess fairness, such as **demographic parity**, **equalized odds**, and **disparate impact**. These metrics help you understand how well your model treats different demographic groups.

- o **Error Analysis**: Analyze model errors to identify if certain groups are being disproportionately affected by poor predictions. For example, a facial recognition system might perform poorly on certain ethnic groups.

- o **Transparency and Interpretability**: Use tools like **LIME, SHAP**, or **Integrated Gradients** to make the model's predictions interpretable. This helps stakeholders understand how the model works and why it makes certain decisions.

4. **Deployment and Monitoring**:

- o **Continuous Monitoring**: After deployment, continuously monitor the model's performance to ensure it continues to operate ethically. This includes checking for any drifts in data or performance that could lead to biased outcomes.

- o **Model Retraining**: Periodically retrain models using fresh data to ensure they remain accurate and fair, especially if the distribution of incoming data changes over time.

- o **Clear Accountability**: Clearly define who is responsible for maintaining and updating the model, and establish processes for accountability if issues arise.

5. **Ethical Guidelines and Frameworks**:

   o **Adopt Ethical AI Principles**: Follow established ethical guidelines for AI development, such as the **EU Ethics Guidelines for Trustworthy AI**, **IEEE Ethically Aligned Design**, or the **OECD Principles on Artificial Intelligence**.

   o **Ethical Audits**: Regularly conduct ethical audits of your models and systems to ensure compliance with fairness, transparency, and accountability principles.

Conclusion

In this chapter, we explored the ethical considerations in machine learning, emphasizing the importance of addressing bias, fairness, transparency, and accountability in the development and deployment of machine learning models. By carefully considering and addressing these issues at every stage of the machine learning lifecycle, we can build models that are not only effective but also ethically responsible.

Ethical machine learning models are critical for ensuring that AI technologies benefit all individuals and communities fairly, without perpetuating harmful biases or discriminatory practices. As machine learning continues to play an increasing role in society, it is essential that data scientists, engineers, and organizations remain vigilant and proactive in building and deploying models that align with ethical principles.

CHAPTER 26

SCALING AND OPTIMIZING MACHINE LEARNING MODELS

Scaling Models for Large Datasets

As the volume of data continues to grow, scaling machine learning models to handle **large datasets** becomes essential for real-world applications. Large datasets can be difficult to process using traditional machine learning methods due to computational constraints such as memory limitations, slow processing speeds, and inefficiencies in training times.

Challenges with Large Datasets:

1. **Memory Consumption**: Storing and processing large datasets often require more memory than is available on a single machine, leading to bottlenecks.
2. **Training Time**: Models trained on large datasets can take hours, days, or even weeks to complete.
3. **Inefficient Algorithms**: Some machine learning algorithms may not scale well with increasing data sizes or may become too slow or inaccurate.

Strategies for Scaling Models:

1. **Data Sampling**:
   - One common approach to scaling is to use **data sampling**, where you train the model on a smaller, representative subset of the data. While this reduces the size of the data used for training, it's essential that the sampled data captures the key characteristics of the entire dataset to avoid bias.

2. **Feature Selection and Dimensionality Reduction**:
   - Reducing the number of features (or dimensions) can significantly improve training efficiency. Techniques such as **Principal Component Analysis (PCA)** or **feature selection methods** can reduce the feature space, speeding up training and reducing computational load.

3. **Online Learning (Incremental Learning)**:
   - **Online learning** allows models to be trained on data in smaller batches or even individual samples. This technique enables the model to update its parameters incrementally as new data arrives, making it well-suited for large or continuously growing datasets. Algorithms like **Stochastic Gradient Descent (SGD)** are commonly used for online learning.

4. **Model Parallelism**:

- o Splitting the training process across multiple machines or cores can allow you to scale the model. **Data parallelism** involves dividing the dataset into smaller chunks, each of which is processed independently, and then combining the results.

5. **Efficient Data Storage and Access**:
   - o Use efficient data storage formats like **Parquet** or **ORC** that are optimized for big data processing. Additionally, distributed databases or data lakes can help store and retrieve large datasets efficiently for model training.

6. **Batch Processing**:
   - o For certain types of models, especially those that process large amounts of data sequentially (like deep learning models), using batch processing techniques can help manage memory and speed up training by processing chunks of data at a time.

Distributed Machine Learning with Hadoop and Spark

When datasets grow too large to fit into a single machine's memory, **distributed machine learning** becomes necessary. Distributed learning involves splitting the training task across multiple machines, allowing the model to be trained in parallel on many subsets of the data.

1. **Hadoop**:
   o **Apache Hadoop** is an open-source framework for distributed storage and processing of large datasets. It uses the **MapReduce** programming model to process data in parallel across many nodes in a cluster.
   o **MapReduce** works by splitting the data into smaller chunks and then mapping a function over the chunks, followed by reducing the results. This can be useful for large-scale data preprocessing and aggregation tasks.
   o **Challenges with Hadoop**:
     ▪ Hadoop is primarily designed for batch processing and might not be ideal for real-time machine learning tasks.
     ▪ It requires a certain level of infrastructure management to deploy and manage clusters.

2. **Apache Spark**:
   o **Apache Spark** is a unified analytics engine for big data processing that is much faster than Hadoop. It supports real-time streaming data and can be used for machine learning tasks using the **MLlib** library.
   o Spark enables **in-memory computing**, which allows it to process large datasets much faster

than Hadoop. It can distribute both the training data and the computation itself, reducing the time required for model training.

- o Spark supports a range of machine learning algorithms and can scale to handle terabytes of data, making it suitable for large-scale machine learning projects.

3. **Distributed Machine Learning Frameworks**:
- o **TensorFlow** and **PyTorch**: These deep learning frameworks support **distributed training** using multi-GPU setups or across multiple machines. TensorFlow uses **TensorFlow Distributed**, and PyTorch offers **DistributedDataParallel** for efficient parallelism.
- o **XGBoost**: An optimized gradient boosting framework that supports distributed computing and can handle large datasets efficiently.

4. **Benefits of Distributed Machine Learning**:
- o **Scalability**: Training on larger datasets is possible without running into memory constraints.
- o **Faster Training**: Parallelization reduces the overall training time.
- o **Fault Tolerance**: Distributed systems can handle node failures and continue training without data loss.

Example: Training a large-scale **random forest** model using **Apache Spark**:

python

```
from pyspark.ml.classification import RandomForestClassifier
from pyspark.ml.feature import VectorAssembler
from pyspark.sql import SparkSession

# Initialize Spark session
spark = SparkSession.builder.appName('RandomForestExample').getOrCreate()

# Load data
data = spark.read.csv('large_dataset.csv', header=True, inferSchema=True)

# Prepare features
assembler = VectorAssembler(inputCols=data.columns[:-1], outputCol="features")
data = assembler.transform(data)

# Split the data
training_data, test_data = data.randomSplit([0.8, 0.2], seed=42)
```

```
# Train a RandomForest model
rf  =  RandomForestClassifier(labelCol="label",
featuresCol="features")
model = rf.fit(training_data)

# Evaluate the model
predictions = model.transform(test_data)
predictions.select("prediction", "label").show()
```

Techniques for Optimizing Training Time

Training large machine learning models on vast datasets can be time-consuming. Optimizing training time while maintaining accuracy is crucial for real-world machine learning applications. Here are several techniques to speed up training:

1. **Data Preprocessing Optimization**:
   o **Efficient Data Loading**: Use efficient data loading and streaming techniques to load and preprocess data in parallel during training. This ensures that data bottlenecks do not slow down the training process.
   o **Data Augmentation**: Instead of training on the entire dataset, use data augmentation techniques like **random cropping**, **rotation**, or **shuffling** to generate more training examples from the existing data.
2. **Use of Hardware Acceleration**:

- o **GPUs** (Graphics Processing Units) and **TPUs** (Tensor Processing Units) are specialized hardware designed to accelerate matrix operations. Leveraging GPUs or TPUs can significantly speed up the training process, especially for deep learning models.

- o **Distributed Training**: For very large models, distributed training across multiple machines or GPUs can reduce training time. This is especially useful in deep learning where model training can be computationally intensive.

3. **Early Stopping**:

- o **Early stopping** is a technique used to stop training once the model's performance stops improving on the validation set. This prevents the model from training unnecessarily for too many epochs and helps to avoid overfitting.

- o **Example**: In neural networks, training may be stopped early if the validation accuracy plateaus or starts to degrade.

4. **Batch Size Optimization**:

- o Adjusting the **batch size** can affect training speed and performance. Larger batch sizes may lead to faster training by utilizing parallelism better but may also consume more memory. Smaller batch sizes may slow down training but may lead to more generalizable models.

- o **Dynamic batching**: Adjust the batch size during training based on system constraints (e.g., GPU memory).

5. **Transfer Learning**:

- o **Transfer learning** involves taking a pre-trained model and fine-tuning it on a new dataset. This reduces training time significantly, especially for deep learning models, as the model already has learned representations from a similar task.
- o This is particularly effective when working with large datasets in domains like image recognition and natural language processing (e.g., using pre-trained models like **BERT** for NLP tasks).

6. **Model Simplification**:

- o **Pruning**: In decision trees, pruning involves cutting down the size of the tree by removing nodes that provide little additional predictive power. In deep learning, pruning can involve removing unnecessary weights or neurons.
- o **Dimensionality Reduction**: Using techniques like **PCA (Principal Component Analysis)** or **autoencoders** to reduce the feature space before training can help speed up the process and improve model performance.

7. **Optimized Algorithms**:

   o Some machine learning algorithms are inherently more computationally efficient than others. For example, **XGBoost** and **LightGBM** are optimized gradient boosting frameworks that are faster and require less memory than traditional models like **Random Forest.**

8. **Asynchronous and Parallelized Training**:

   o **Asynchronous SGD (Stochastic Gradient Descent)** allows updates to be performed without waiting for all machines to complete their work, which can speed up convergence in distributed settings.

   o **Data Parallelism**: Training can be parallelized by distributing different subsets of the dataset across multiple machines or GPUs.

Conclusion

In this chapter, we discussed how to scale and optimize machine learning models to handle large datasets. We covered **distributed machine learning** using frameworks like **Hadoop** and **Spark**, and we explored techniques for optimizing training time, such as using **hardware acceleration**, **batch optimization**, and **early stopping**.

By implementing these techniques, you can build scalable machine learning models that handle vast amounts of data efficiently, while also reducing training time and computational costs. As the size of datasets continues to grow, mastering these techniques will be essential for deploying machine learning models in real-world applications.

CHAPTER 27

FUTURE OF MACHINE LEARNING AND AI

Current Trends in Machine Learning

Machine learning (ML) and artificial intelligence (AI) are rapidly evolving fields that continue to make significant strides across various industries. As technology advances, several key trends are emerging that shape the future of ML and AI. Below are some of the current trends in the field:

1. **Deep Learning Advancements**:
   - **Definition**: Deep learning, a subset of machine learning, has made huge strides, especially in areas such as **image recognition**, **natural language processing**, and **speech recognition**. The development of more sophisticated architectures (like **Transformers** and **Generative Adversarial Networks (GANs)**) has enabled major breakthroughs.
   - **Applications**: Self-driving cars, facial recognition systems, medical imaging, and natural language generation are among the areas where deep learning is having the most impact.

- o **Trends**: More efficient deep learning models, such as **BERT** (Bidirectional Encoder Representations from Transformers) and **GPT** (Generative Pretrained Transformer), are becoming more widely used, enabling sophisticated language models for tasks like sentiment analysis, translation, and conversational agents.

2. **Transfer Learning**:

- o **Definition**: Transfer learning involves taking a pre-trained model on one task and fine-tuning it on a new task with limited data. This allows for faster training and more effective use of data.

- o **Applications**: Transfer learning is particularly useful in fields like computer vision and NLP, where pre-trained models (like **ResNet** for image classification or **GPT-3** for text generation) can be adapted for specific use cases without needing vast amounts of new data.

3. **Explainable AI (XAI)**:

- o **Definition**: **Explainable AI** refers to methods that make machine learning models more interpretable, providing insights into how decisions are made. This is particularly important for industries where transparency is required, such as healthcare, finance, and legal systems.

- o **Trend**: With more complex models (like deep learning) becoming prevalent, the demand for **interpretable models** that offer understandable explanations of their predictions is increasing. Techniques like **SHAP** (Shapley Additive Explanations) and **LIME** (Local Interpretable Model-agnostic Explanations) are gaining traction to help make models more explainable.

4. **AutoML (Automated Machine Learning)**:
    - o **Definition**: AutoML refers to the automation of the process of applying machine learning models to real-world problems. It involves automating tasks such as data preprocessing, model selection, and hyperparameter tuning.
    - o **Trend**: With the growing demand for AI, but the shortage of skilled data scientists, AutoML tools like **Google AutoML** and **H2O.ai** are making it easier for businesses and non-experts to deploy machine learning models, enabling **democratization** of AI.

5. **Federated Learning**:
    - o **Definition**: **Federated learning** is a method of machine learning where the model is trained across multiple decentralized devices or servers without sharing the actual data. This allows for data privacy, as the model learns on each device

and only shares the model weights (updates), not the data.

- o **Trend**: With increasing concerns about data privacy and regulations like the **General Data Protection Regulation (GDPR)**, federated learning is becoming an essential method for training models in scenarios where data privacy is paramount, such as mobile devices or healthcare applications.

6. **AI in Healthcare**:

- o **Applications**: AI has proven transformative in healthcare, from disease diagnosis using medical images (like **radiology**) to personalized treatment recommendations using patient data. AI models are also used for drug discovery and patient monitoring in real-time.

- o **Trend**: AI and machine learning are expected to further transform healthcare, with an increased focus on **predictive healthcare**, where machine learning models help predict patient conditions before they become critical.

7. **Ethical AI**:

- o **Trend**: As AI technologies become more widespread, ethical concerns related to AI and machine learning, including bias, fairness, and accountability, have come to the forefront. More regulations and frameworks are emerging to ensure AI is developed and used responsibly, ethically, and transparently.

- o **Applications**: Companies are incorporating ethical considerations into their AI systems to ensure fairness, privacy, and equity. This includes tools for detecting **bias in models** and implementing transparent decision-making processes.

Emerging Technologies: Autonomous Systems, Edge AI, etc.

Machine learning is not only evolving in traditional areas like cloud computing and data centers, but is also paving the way for **emerging technologies** that bring new capabilities and opportunities. Here are a few key technologies that will shape the future:

1. **Autonomous Systems**:
    - o **Definition**: Autonomous systems refer to machines that can perform tasks or make decisions without human intervention. These systems rely heavily on machine learning, computer vision, and reinforcement learning.
    - o **Applications**: Self-driving cars, drones, autonomous robots, and automated industrial systems.

- o **Trend**: The development of autonomous vehicles, drones, and robots is accelerating, with real-world applications in delivery services, agriculture, and transportation. Machine learning models are at the core of enabling these systems to make real-time, data-driven decisions.

2. **Edge AI**:

- o **Definition**: **Edge AI** refers to performing machine learning computations on devices (such as smartphones, IoT devices, and sensors) rather than sending data to the cloud. This allows for **real-time** processing with minimal latency and reduced dependency on internet connectivity.

- o **Applications**: Autonomous vehicles, smart cities, industrial IoT, healthcare devices, and wearable tech.

- o **Trend**: With advancements in hardware (e.g., **Edge TPUs** and **NVIDIA Jetson**), AI models are being deployed on edge devices to make real-time decisions. This reduces data transfer, improves privacy, and supports low-latency applications.

3. **Quantum Computing and AI**:

- o **Definition**: Quantum computing is an emerging technology that leverages the principles of quantum mechanics to perform calculations much faster than classical computers. Machine learning models, especially those with complex optimization problems, can benefit from quantum computing by drastically reducing computation times.

- o **Trend**: Researchers are exploring how quantum computers can be used to enhance machine learning algorithms, especially for tasks like **optimization, pattern recognition**, and **large-scale simulations**.

4. **AI and Robotics**:
   - o **Applications**: Robots powered by AI are being used for various tasks, from warehouse automation (e.g., **Amazon robots**) to medical surgery (e.g., **robotic-assisted surgery**).
   - o **Trend**: As AI and robotics continue to converge, we are likely to see an increase in autonomous robots capable of more complex tasks, improving productivity and enhancing capabilities in industries like manufacturing, logistics, and healthcare.

How to Continue Your Machine Learning Journey Beyond This Book

Machine learning is a vast and constantly evolving field, and this book is just the beginning of your learning journey. Here are several ways you can continue building your machine learning skills:

1. **Online Courses and Certifications**:
   o **Coursera**: Offers comprehensive courses from top universities, such as **Andrew Ng's Machine Learning** course and **Deep Learning Specialization**.
   o **edX**: Offers courses on AI and machine learning from institutions like MIT and Harvard.
   o **Udacity**: Provides nanodegrees and specialized programs like **AI for Robotics** and **Deep Learning**.
   o **Kaggle**: Kaggle provides **hands-on challenges** and learning resources where you can practice solving machine learning problems and competing with others.

2. **Research Papers and Journals**:
   o Reading **research papers** is a great way to stay updated on the latest advancements in machine learning. Websites like **arXiv.org** and **Google Scholar** provide access to cutting-edge research papers.
   o Join platforms like **ACM (Association for Computing Machinery)** or **IEEE** to read academic journals on AI and machine learning.

3. **Participating in Competitions**:

- o **Kaggle** competitions provide an excellent opportunity to apply your skills to real-world problems. By participating in these competitions, you can learn from others, improve your modeling techniques, and even win prizes.
- o Competitions also allow you to develop skills in areas like **data preprocessing**, **model evaluation**, and **model deployment**.

4. **Books and Documentation**:
   - o Read advanced machine learning books to deepen your understanding:
     - **"Deep Learning" by Ian Goodfellow, Yoshua Bengio, and Aaron Courville**: An authoritative text on deep learning.
     - **"Pattern Recognition and Machine Learning" by Christopher Bishop**: A comprehensive guide to statistical learning.
   - o Explore the official documentation of machine learning libraries like **TensorFlow**, **PyTorch**, **Scikit-learn**, and **Keras** to understand their capabilities and best practices.

5. **Work on Personal Projects**:
   - o Hands-on experience is key to mastering machine learning. Work on personal projects that interest you, whether it's a recommendation system,

sentiment analysis tool, or image classifier. Start small, and gradually work on more complex systems.

- ○ Contribute to **open-source projects** in machine learning to collaborate with the community and gain exposure to real-world applications.

6. **Join the AI Community**:

- ○ Participate in **machine learning meetups, AI conferences**, and **hackathons** to connect with like-minded people, share ideas, and learn from industry experts.

- ○ Engage with communities like **Reddit (r/MachineLearning)**, **StackOverflow**, and **GitHub** to ask questions, discuss challenges, and share knowledge.

Conclusion

Machine learning and AI are rapidly advancing fields with significant implications for businesses, society, and individuals. In this chapter, we explored the **current trends in machine learning**, the **emerging technologies** shaping the future of AI, and how you can continue your learning journey. As AI becomes more integrated into everyday life, the opportunities for machine learning professionals are vast and growing. By staying curious, engaging with the community, and continuously learning, you will be well-equipped to contribute to this exciting field and shape its future.